16LIVES

THOMAS CLARKE

The 16LIVES Series

JAMES CONNOLLY Lorcan Collins

MICHAEL MALLIN Brian Hughes

JOSEPH PLUNKETT Honor O Brolchain

EDWARD DALY Helen Litton

SEÁN HEUSTON John Gibney

ROGER CASEMENT Angus Mitchell

SEÁN MACDIARMADA Brian Feeney

THOMAS CLARKE Helen Litton

ÉAMONN CEANNT Mary Gallagher

WILLIE PEARSE Róisín Ní Ghairbhí

THOMAS MACDONAGH Shane Kenna

JOHN MACBRIDE Donal Fallon

THOMAS KENT Meda Ryan

CON COLBERT John O'Callaghan

MICHAEL O'HANRAHAN Conor Kostick

HELEN LITTON – AUTHOR OF 16LIVES: THOMAS CLARKE

Helen Litton, freelance indexer and editor, has written a series of illustrated histories and edited *Kathleen Clarke: Revolutionary Woman*, an autobiography (1991). Helen's paternal grandmother was Laura Daly O'Sullivan of Limerick, sister of Kathleen Daly, the wife of Thomas Clarke and of Commandant Edward Daly, whose biography Helen has written in the *16 Lives* series.

LORCAN COLLINS – SERIES EDITOR

Lorcan Collins was born and raised in Dublin. A lifelong interest in Irish history led to the foundation of his hugely-popular 1916 Walking Tour in 1996. He co-authored *The Easter Rising: A Guide to Dublin in 1916* (O'Brien Press, 2000) with Conor Kostick. His biography of James Connolly was published in the *16 Lives* series in 2012. He is also a regular contributor to radio, television and historical journals. *16 Lives* is Lorcan's concept and he is co-editor of the series.

DR RUÁN O'DONNELL – SERIES EDITOR

Dr Ruán O'Donnell is a senior lecturer at the University of Limerick. A graduate of University College Dublin and the Australian National University, O'Donnell has published extensively on Irish Republicanism. Titles include *Robert Emmet and the Rising of 1803*, *The Impact of 1916* (editor), *Special Category, The IRA in English prisons 1968–1978* and *The O'Brien Pocket History of the Irish Famine*. He is a director of the Irish Manuscripts Commission and a frequent contributor to the national and international media on the subject of Irish revolutionary history.

● ●

16LIVES

THOMAS CLARKE

Helen Litton

THE O'BRIEN PRESS
DUBLIN

First published 2014 by
The O'Brien Press Ltd,
12 Terenure Road East, Rathgar,
Dublin 6, Ireland.
Tel: +353 1 4923333; Fax: +353 1 4922777
E-mail: books@obrien.ie.
Website: www.obrien.ie
ISBN: 978-1-84717-261-7
Text © copyright Helen Litton 2014
Copyright for typesetting, layout, editing, design
© The O'Brien Press Ltd
Series concept: Lorcan Collins

8 7 6 5 4 3 2 1
18 17 16 15 14
All quotations have been reproduced with original spelling and punctuation. Errors are author's own.

Printed and bound by CPI Group (UK) Ltd, Croydon, CR0 4YY
The paper used in this book is produced using pulp from managed forests.

PICTURE CREDITS

The author and publisher thank the following for permission to use photographs and illustrative material: front cover image: Courtesy of the National Library of Ireland (NLI); back cover: Helen Litton/O'Sullivan Family, Limerick; inside front cover: Helen Litton. National Archives of Ireland: section 1, p2; Helen Litton/O'Sullivan Family, Limerick: section 1, p1 both, p3 both, p4, p5 all, p6, p7 both, p8 bottom, section 2, p1 top, p4, p5, p8; Lorcan Collins: section 1, p8 top, section 2, p2 top; National Museum Collins Barracks: section 2, p1 bottom; Courtesy of Kilmainham Gaol Museum: section 2, p2 bottom, p3 both; NLI: section 2, p7; Clarke Collection, John J Burns Library, Boston College: section 2, p6.
If any involuntary infringement of copyright has ocurred, sincere apologies are offered and the owners of such copyright are requested to contact the publisher.

DEDICATION

For Frank

ACKNOWLEDGEMENTS

I am grateful to The O'Brien Press for giving me the opportunity to write this contribution to the study of Tom Clarke, a relatively neglected leader of the Easter Rising. I particularly thank my editor, Mary Webb, for her patience, and the series editors, Lorcan Collins and Ruán O'Donnell.

Thanks are due to the following: Bill Hurley, archivist of the American Irish Historical Association, New York; The Bureau of Military History, Dublin; Siobháin de hÓir, of Dublin, who lent me her father-in-law Éamonn's unpublished memoirs; the staff of the Brooklyn Public Library, New York; the staff of the John J Burns Library, Boston College; the staff of the Archives Department, University College Dublin; the staff of the National Library of Ireland. Thanks are also due to Linda Clayton, Association of Professional Genealogists in Ireland, for research into the Clarke family.

I am grateful to my husband Frank, Anthony and Kristen, Eleanor and Jim and our grandchildren Aoife and Aidan for all their help and support, and to all family and friends for listening to my moans about 'too much material and not enough time'. Above all, I am deeply grateful to my uncle and aunt Edward and Laura Daly O'Sullivan, and my cousins Nóra and Mairéad de hÓir, all of Limerick, whose parents fought during the Easter Rising and who shared memories and anecdotes with me.

Finally, I pay tribute to my colleagues of 'Concerned Relatives of Signatories to the Proclamation' – Eamonn Ceannt, James Connolly Heron, Muriel McAuley, Pat MacDermott, Honor Ó Brolcháin, Lucille Redmond and Noel Scarlett. Along with other groups, we have been working to preserve the footprint of the retreat and surrender of the Easter Rising, all under threat of demolition. We are grateful that the National Monument of Nos 14–17 Moore Street has recently been reprieved by James Deenihan, Minister for Arts, Heritage and the Gaeltacht, and we hope to see this whole 'battlefield' secured and preserved for the centenary of the Easter Rising in 2016.

16LIVES Timeline

1845–51. The Great Hunger in Ireland. One million people die and over the next decades millions more emigrate.

1858, March 17. The Irish Republican Brotherhood, or Fenians, are formed with the express intention of overthrowing British rule in Ireland by whatever means necessary.

1867, February and March. Fenian Uprising.

1870, May. Home Rule movement founded by Isaac Butt, who had previously campaigned for amnesty for Fenian prisoners.

1879–81. The Land War. Violent agrarian agitation against English landlords.

1884, November 1. The Gaelic Athletic Association founded – immediately infiltrated by the Irish Republican Brotherhood (IRB).

1893, July 31. Gaelic League founded by Douglas Hyde and Eoin MacNeill. The *Gaelic Revival*, a period of Irish Nationalism, pride in the language, history, culture and sport.

1900, September. *Cumann na nGaedheal* (Irish Council) founded by Arthur Griffith.

1905–07. *Cumann na nGaedheal*, the Dungannon Clubs and the National Council are amalgamated to form *Sinn Féin* (We Ourselves).

1909, August. Countess Markievicz and Bulmer Hobson organise nationalist youths into *Na Fianna Éireann* (Warriors of Ireland) a kind of boy scout brigade.

1912, April. Asquith introduces the Third Home Rule Bill to the British Parliament. Passed by the Commons and rejected by the Lords, the Bill would have to become law due to the Parliament Act. Home Rule expected to be introduced for Ireland by autumn 1914.

1913, January. Sir Edward Carson and James Craig set up Ulster Volunteer Force (UVF) with the intention of defending Ulster against Home Rule.

1913. Jim Larkin, founder of the Irish Transport and General Workers' Union (ITGWU) calls for a workers' strike for better pay and conditions.

1913, August 31. Jim Larkin speaks at a banned rally on Sackville (O'Connell) Street; Bloody Sunday.

1913, November 23. James Connolly, Jack White and Jim Larkin establish the Irish Citizen Army (ICA) in order to protect strikers.

1913, November 25. The Irish Volunteers founded in Dublin to 'secure the rights and liberties common to all the people of Ireland'.

1914, March 20. Resignations of British officers force British government not to use British army to enforce Home Rule, an event known as the 'Curragh Mutiny'.

1914, April 2. In Dublin, Agnes O'Farrelly, Mary MacSwiney, Countess Markievicz and others establish Cumann na mBan as a women's volunteer force dedicated to establishing Irish freedom and assisting the Irish Volunteers.

1914, April 24. A shipment of 35,000 rifles and five million rounds of ammunition is landed at Larne for the UVF.

1914, July 26. Irish Volunteers unload a shipment of 900 rifles and 45,000 rounds of ammunition shipped from Germany aboard Erskine Childers' yacht, the *Asgard*. British troops fire on crowd on Bachelors Walk, Dublin. Three citizens are killed.

1914, August 4. Britain declares war on Germany. Home Rule for Ireland shelved for the duration of the First World War.

1914, September 9. Meeting held at Gaelic League headquarters between IRB and other extreme republicans. Initial decision made to stage an uprising while Britain is at war.

1914, September. 170,000 leave the Volunteers and form the National Volunteers or Redmondites. Only 11,000 remain as the Irish Volunteers under Eóin Mac-Neill.

1915, May–September. Military Council of the IRB is formed.

1915, August 1. Pearse gives fiery oration at the funeral of Jeremiah O'Donovan Rossa.

1916, January 19–22. James Connolly joins the IRB Military Council, thus ensuring that the ICA shall be involved in the Rising. Rising date confirmed for Easter.

1916, April 20, 4.15pm. *The Aud* arrives at Tralee Bay, laden with 20,000 German rifles for the Rising. Captain Karl Spindler waits in vain for a signal from shore.

1916, April 21, 2.15am. Roger Casement and his two companions go ashore from U-19 and land on Banna Strand. Casement is arrested at McKenna's Fort.

6.30pm. *The Aud* is captured by the British navy and forced to sail towards Cork Harbour.

22 April, 9.30am. *The Aud* is scuttled by her captain off Daunt's Rock.

10pm. Eóin MacNeill as chief-of-staff of the Irish Volunteers issues the countermanding order in Dublin to try to stop the Rising.

1916, April 23, 9am, Easter Sunday. The Military Council meets to discuss the situation, considering MacNeill has placed an advertisement in a Sunday newspaper halting all Volunteer operations. The Rising is put on hold for twenty-four hours. Hundreds of copies of *The Proclamation of the Republic* are printed in Liberty Hall.

1916, April 24, 12 noon, Easter Monday. The Rising begins in Dublin.

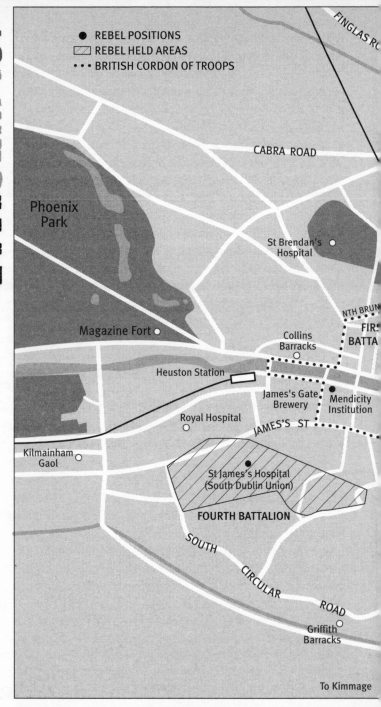

16 LIVES MAP

Legend:
- ● REBEL POSITIONS
- ▨ REBEL HELD AREAS
- ••• BRITISH CORDON OF TROOPS

FINGLAS RO

CABRA ROAD

Phoenix Park

St Brendan's Hospital ○

Magazine Fort ○

NTH BRUN

FIRS
BATTA

Collins Barracks ○

Heuston Station

James's Gate Brewery ●
Mendicity Institution ●

Royal Hospital ○

JAMES'S ST

Kilmainham Gaol ○

St James's Hospital (South Dublin Union) ●

FOURTH BATTALION

SOUTH

CIRCULAR

ROAD

Griffith Barracks ○

To Kimmage

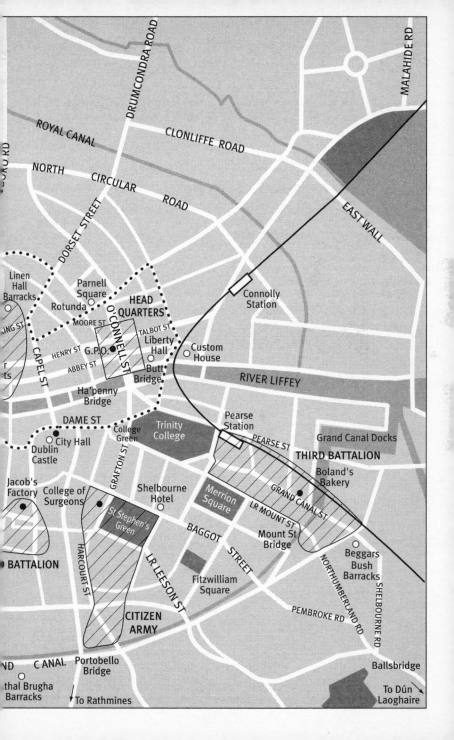

16LIVES – Series Introduction

This book is part of a series called *16 LIVES*, conceived with the objective of recording for posterity the lives of the sixteen men who were executed after the 1916 Easter Rising. Who were these people and what drove them to commit themselves to violent revolution?

The rank and file as well as the leadership were all from diverse backgrounds. Some were privileged and some had no material wealth. Some were highly educated writers, poets or teachers and others had little formal schooling. Their common desire, to set Ireland on the road to national freedom, united them under the one banner of the army of the Irish Republic. They occupied key buildings in Dublin and around Ireland for one week before they were forced to surrender. The leaders were singled out for harsh treatment and all sixteen men were executed for their role in the Rising.

Meticulously researched yet written in an accessible fashion, the *16 LIVES* biographies can be read as individual volumes but together they make a highly collectible series.

Lorcan Collins & Dr Ruán O'Donnell,
16 Lives *Series Editors*

CONTENTS

Chapter One

The Early Years
1858-83

'In a sense, Tom Clarke is a man of one small book, a few letters, and his signature in the 1916 Proclamation.'

This remark by historian Desmond Ryan (who had fought in the GPO) sums up the public image of Tom Clarke.[1] A born conspirator, always behind the scenes, Clarke was overshadowed in Easter Rising legend by more charismatic and eloquent figures such as Patrick Pearse, James Connolly and Joseph Plunkett. In recent years new material has become available, and deeper research has begun to alter received ideas about this unassuming-looking man, and to emphasise his absolutely central role in the history of the Rising and the years leading up to it.

Tom Clarke had a somewhat unusual background for an Irish revolutionary, who was to become one of Ireland's most celebrated rebel leaders. English-born, he had a father whose career was spent in the British Army, and who wanted his son to follow suit.

Tom's father James, from Errew townland, Carrigallen, County Leitrim, was born in 1830 to James Clarke (or Clerkin), who shared a small farm with his brother Owen, although in his son's marriage certificate James senior is described as a 'labourer'. The family was Protestant. When James the younger left school, he worked as a groom, then enlisted as a cavalry soldier on 4 December 1847 in Ballyshannon, County Donegal. His age was given as 17 years and 11 months; he was just under proper age for the army – eighteen – so his first month of service was not counted towards the final total on his discharge.[2] He had decided on an army career during the worst years of the Great Famine, when opportunities of employment were few, and a small farm would not have supported a family; his experience with horses made the cavalry a suitable choice for him.

James's regiment was sent to join the Crimean War (1853-6), in which the English, French and Turks united to fight Russia. This war is mostly remembered now for the Charge of the Light Brigade, and the development of Florence Nightingale's theories of nursing care. According to his military record, James saw action at the famous battles of Alma, Balaklava and Inkerman in 1854, and the year-long siege of Sebastopol (September 1854–September 1855). He received a medal for the Crimean War, with 'clasps' for the three battles and the siege.

He was later garrisoned in Clonmel, County Tipperary, probably on his return from the Crimean War. Here he met Mary Palmer, from Clogheen, and although she was a Catholic, they were married on 31 May 1857 at Shanrahan Church of Ireland parish church, County Tipperary. The marriage record describes her as 'of full age' (meaning over 21); her father was Michael Palmer, a labourer.[3] Her mother's maiden name was Kew, and she had obviously been very well-known in her community. According to some anonymous 'notes' for a life of Tom Clarke, Mrs Palmer's funeral in the 1880s (in either Clonmel or Clogheen) was a big public occasion, and she was the first woman waked in the local Catholic church.[4]

Soon after the marriage James was transferred to Hurst Castle, Hampshire, England, and here their first child, Thomas James Clarke, was born, on 11 March 1858.[5] He was baptised a Catholic; the couple obviously came to some agreement on this, or perhaps James was not too concerned about such matters. Catholics marrying Protestants were obliged to rear their children as Catholics.

James must have left the cavalry, because he was now promoted to Bombardier (the lowest rank of non-commissioned officer) in the Royal Artillery in October 1857. He was promoted further, to Corporal, in 1859, and transferred to the 12th Brigade of the Royal Regiment of Artillery. On 9 April 1859, he was sent to South Africa. According to Louis

Le Roux, who wrote the first authorised biography of Tom Clarke, the little family 'narrowly escaped drowning during the voyage when the ship on which they were travelling became involved in a serious collision'.[6] A note among the Clarke Papers in the National Library of Ireland says that it was a collision with a coal boat.[7]

The family spent almost six years in South Africa, in various garrisons. The English and the Dutch South Africans (Boers) had been at loggerheads over the ownership of the province since the late 18th century, as it was an important stop on the trade-routes from Europe to India. The Clarke family was living in Natal when Tom's sister, Maria Jane, was born on 23 December 1859, and young Tom began attending school there. Natal, annexed by the British from the Boers in 1845, had been separated from the colony in 1856, and granted its own autonomous institutions. It was later one of the four provinces of the Union of South Africa, established in 1910.

James was promoted to Battery Sergeant at the end of 1859, in the Cape of Good Hope. He then re-engaged himself for a period of nine years, starting on 21 March 1860. He and his family returned to Ireland in March 1865, and James was appointed Sergeant of the Ulster Militia. Its headquarters were in Charlemont Castle, County Tyrone. As the barracks accommodation was inadequate to house a growing family, the family moved into Anne Street in Dungannon, the nearby town.

A son, Michael, was born to James and Mary Clarke, in Clogheen, County Tipperary, Mary's native place, on 9 May 1865. The birth was registered by Bridget Palmer. His father is described as a soldier, 'resident in Portsmouth'. Mary, who must have travelled from South Africa while pregnant, had probably gone to stay with her family while James, temporarily based in England, arranged the move to Dungannon. Michael must not have lived very long, as he is not part of the family history, but no official record of his death can be found.

James and Mary's second daughter, Hannah Palmer Clarke, was born in Dungannon on 24 August 1868, and on 26 December of that year James Clarke, Soldier No. 694, claimed his discharge from army service. The record states, 'Discharge proposed in consequence of his having claimed it on termination of his second period of limited engagement'. James had served for 21 years and nine days, and his discharge was approved, and carried out at Gosport. On 12 January 1869, he was admitted as an out-pensioner of the Royal Hospital, Chelsea, London, aged 39, on a pension of one shilling and 11 pence per day. This was later increased to two shillings and eight pence per day.

He is described in his discharge papers as of swarthy complexion, with dark eyes and hair, with no marks or scars, and 5 feet 7 and a half inches in height. The papers note that his behaviour has been 'Very Good'. He had two Good Conduct Badges before his first promotion to Bombardier; he had no entries in the regimental 'Defaulters' Book', and had never been tried by court martial.[8]

The day after his discharge, 13 January, his records state that he was appointed a Sergeant on the permanent staff of the 6th Brigade, Northern Ireland Division, and the family remained in Dungannon. [9] Here Alfred Edward was born, on 24 May 1870, in Anne Street. James is described as 'Sergeant, Tyrone Artillery'. A further birth took place, that of Joseph George, on 16 November 1874; the family was now living in Northland Row. Sadly, Joseph George died on 22 November, having suffered convulsions. His death was registered by James Clarke.[10]

Tom Clarke was eight years old when his family came to Dungannon, and thus spent almost all of his formative years in the town. A bright boy, he attended St Patrick's National School. His first teacher was Francis Daly, followed by Cornelius Collins, who employed Tom as an assistant teacher or 'monitor'. Le Roux says this continued until the school closed in 1881, but Tom had left for the USA in 1880.[11] Tom was restless and energetic, and it seemed unlikely that he would remain a schoolteacher for long. A later witness statement says that he failed to move higher than a monitor when he refused to teach Catechism on Sunday mornings. 'He had no objection to teaching Catechism, but reckoned that Sunday was not included in a teacher's working week.'[12]

Tom's best friend was William or Billy Kelly, who assisted Louis Le Roux with his biography of Tom, and also left his own memoir.[13]

Dungannon, a linen and brickmaking town with a population of about 4,000 in 1881, provided a microcosm of social conditions in Ulster.[14] The industries were owned and run by Protestants, and employment for Catholics was limited. There was a clear demarcation between the prosperous homes of Protestants, and the areas where Catholics lived in dreadful conditions, in mud cabins outside the town or tenements within it, and where tuberculosis was rife. Riots between Catholics and Protestants were frequent, when one side would attack the other's parades or religious processions.

The town had been a focus of reform activity in February 1782, when the Dungannon Convention took place. This gathering of delegates from Volunteer militia corps was looking for parliamentary reform, and drew up a list of demands for government, the 'Dungannon Resolutions'. The delegates were mostly Protestant, but the thirteenth resolution welcomed a recent relaxation in the Penal Laws which had given more legal rights to Catholics. This movement ultimately led to the establishment, in April 1782, of an independent parliament for Ireland, known as 'Grattan's Parliament'. Dungannon's contribution to legislative freedom made it a gathering-point for local nationalist activity during the nineteenth century. The Fenians or Irish Republican Brotherhood (IRB) were reorganising and recruiting after two abortive rebellions in 1865 and 1867, and Dungannon had its own District Circle of the IRB.

Tom Clarke, witnessing the inequality and discrimination around him, came to the conclusion that British rule was destroying Ireland, and must be cast off. He was drawn more and more to republicanism, and rejected his father's plan that he should join the British Army. James Clarke, according to Le Roux, 'regarded the British Army with superstitious awe, as an unconquerable force, and as the guardian of an unique civilization'. Another statement says that Tom's father had told him he would be knocking against a stone wall if he tried to fight Britain. 'Tom Clarke said he would knock away in the hope that some day the wall would give, and in that he forecast the life of poverty, endurance, hardship and singlemindedness that was to be his.'[15]

The Dungannon District Circle of the IRB met under cover of the Catholic and Total Abstinence Reading Rooms and Dramatic Club. Tom was an active member of this club, but not yet a member of the IRB, when in 1878, when Tom was twenty-one years old, Dungannon was visited by John Daly. Daly, from Limerick, had taken part in the Fenian rising of 1867, and subsequently escaped to America, returning to Ireland in 1869 as a full-time IRB organiser. The IRB was growing, and would soon be an important force within the Land League, the movement for land reform. It would also have some dealings with the Irish Parliamentary Party and its leader, Charles Stewart Parnell. By the mid-1880s it had almost 40,000 members, and 10,000 firearms.

Daly addressed the local IRB groups on Drumco Hill, outside the town. Tom was greatly impressed by him, and resolved to join the IRB. According to Louis Le Roux, he did so in 1882 when, his teaching career having ended, he travelled to Dublin with Billy Kelly and Louis McMullen, his closest friends. The O'Connell Monument, a massive statue to honour Daniel O'Connell, the nineteenth-century lawyer and politician who had espoused non-violent politics and achieved Catholic Emancipation, was to be unveiled in Sackville Street (now O'Connell Street) with great ceremony. On August 14, the day before the unveiling, says Le Roux, John Daly swore Tom Clarke, Billy Kelly and four others from Dungannon into the IRB.

This story cannot be correct; when the O'Connell Monument was unveiled in 1882, Tom and his friends had already been in America for two years. They probably travelled to Dublin in 1879 or 1880, and were sworn into the IRB at that time. Billy Kelly does describe them as travelling for the O'Connell Monument unveiling, but he gives the date of this trip as 1879, and says they met John Daly and Michael Davitt, an ex-IRB man who devoted himself to the cause of land reform.

They travelled to Dublin as members of the Reading

Rooms and Dramatic Club, which had organised the excursion. Tom seems to have been quite active on the drama side of the club: 'The fame of his performance as "Danny Boy" in Dion Boucicault's "Colleen Bawn" reached Dublin, and Tom refused an invitation by Hubert O'Grady, then a famous actor-manager, to join his touring company'.[16] But Tom's interests lay elsewhere; he was appointed First District Secretary of the Dungannon IRB Circle soon after joining it. The Dramatic Club probably served as a good cover for his activities; his father would undoubtedly have disapproved of them, and might even have betrayed him. Tom later laughed over his efforts at acting; he never took it very seriously, but much of his later life required him to act the part of a harmless little shopkeeper, and he did it very successfully.[17]

John Daly, who travelled Ireland advising and encouraging IRB groups under cover of being a commercial traveller, visited Dungannon again, probably in 1879. He advised the Tyrone IRB on drilling, training and arming, so that they could defend themselves and others against the activities of the Royal Irish Constabulary (RIC).

A defining moment in Tom Clarke's life took place in a sectarian context, when a Catholic 'Lady Day' parade, celebrating the Feast of the Assumption, took place on 15 August 1880. The parade was attacked by a crowd of Protestants, and stones were thrown at the RIC. The Riot Act was read, and the police then opened fire on the crowd with live ammunition. One man died and twenty-seven were injured; the police suffered one casualty.[18] Louis Le Roux refers to this as the 'buckshot riot', as buckshot was fired into the crowd. He then says that one young man, who bore a resemblance to Clarke, was arrested on suspicion of having fired on the police during the riot. When this man was able to prove an alibi, the police began to focus on Clarke himself, who had to lie low for a while.

However, Billy Kelly's memoir says that on the night following the 'buckshot riot', eleven RIC men were ambushed by members of the IRB, who included Clarke and Kelly. The police were fired on, and escaped into a public house in Anne Street. When reinforcements arrived, the attackers had to retreat. This was not reported in the press.[19]

One way or another, Clarke and his friends were being noticed, and would be better off elsewhere. The decision was made to emigrate to the United States, and on 29 August 1880 a farewell party was held for several young men who were to leave, among them Billy Kelly. Billy was the only one who knew that Clarke intended to travel with them; Tom had not told his parents. As the young men left for the train to Derry, from where they would sail, Tom went home with his family. That night, he slipped out when all were asleep, and made his own way to Derry.

Le Roux says that the boat on which the friends had been booked needed repairs, and they were stuck in Derry for two weeks, receiving two shillings a day detention money from the shipping company. 'They had a jolly time, making occasional outings on a horse jaunting car, sometimes to Newtowncunningham, in the neighbouring county of Donegal, sometimes as far as Letterkenny.'[20]

It is perhaps odd that his parents did not catch up with him during this enforced holiday, but they must have had a fairly good idea where he had gone, and his father probably felt they were better off without this trouble-making son. Clarke was now twenty-three years of age, old enough to look after himself.

Clarke and his friends finally took ship on an old cattle boat, the *Scandinavia*, belonging to the Allen Line. One story says that there was a mutiny on board the boat during the journey, but they ultimately landed safely at Boston, and travelled on to New York by boat.[21] Clarke and Kelly lodged in Chatham Street, at the house of Patrick O'Connor, who was from County Tyrone. They worked in his shoe store to begin with, and slept in a stone cellar.

After about two months in O'Connor's store, Clarke began work as a night porter at the Mansion House Hotel, Brooklyn, 'where his heaviest duty was to light fifty fires'. The owner, Mr Avery, was establishing a chain of hotels, and found Irish emigrants to be hard-working and honest. He also gave work to Billy Kelly, and promoted Clarke to foreman. However, Avery then sold out to a Dutchman, who sent Kelly to the Garden City Hotel, twenty miles away.

Both Clarke and Kelly had, of course, an introduction to Clan na Gael from the IRB. Clan na Gael had been founded in New York in 1867 by Jerome J. Collins, and it recognised the Supreme Council of the IRB as the government of the Irish Republic 'virtually established'. Many IRB men who were forced out of Ireland or England joined the Clan on arrival in the USA.

Clarke and Kelly arrived at Clan na Gael's Napper Tandy Club, or 'Camp No. 1', at 4 Union Street, introduced by Pat O'Connor, their first employer, and sworn in by Seumas Connolly, Senior Guardian. Tom proved himself keen and energetic, and was soon made Recording Secretary by the 'bosses', Alexander Sullivan, Timothy O'Riordan and Connolly. In 1924 John Kenny, who was president of the club at the time, remembered Tom Clarke as a 'bright, earnest, wiry, alert young fellow'.[22] According to Kelly, the purpose of the club was to instruct its members in the use of explosives, under the tutelage of Dr Thomas Gallagher. 'Lessons' included trips to Staten Island to experiment on rocks with nitroglycerine. When a call went out for 'single men' as volunteers for dangerous work for Ireland, Clarke and Kelly both volunteered, and joined Dr Gallagher's classes.[23] However, when he moved to Garden City, Kelly could no longer attend meetings, although he continued to send his subscriptions.[24]

John Devoy, who had been an organiser for the IRB until the rising of 1865, was also a member of this club. Arrested and imprisoned in 1866, he had been released in 1871 on condition of exile, and joined Clan na Gael in the US, building it up to a strong organisation.

During his time in New York, Clarke would no doubt have been an active participant at Clan na Gael's annual events, such as their Annual Picnic and Gaelic Games each summer, at which dancing was kept up all night, and the celebration of Robert Emmet's birthday on 4 March each year.[25] The Emmet celebrations usually took the form of a mass meeting, at which vehement sentiments were uttered in relation to Britain. One particular meeting resolved 'That British rule in Ireland is without moral or legal sanction, and does not bind in conscience upon Irishmen one moment longer than that which finds them prepared to cast it off'.[26]

In 1867 a technological breakthrough had taken place in the field of explosives. Alfred Nobel, a Swedish chemist, took out a patent for 'dynamite', an explosive which, it was noted, would 'level the playing field for terrorists who wished to strike against the state'.[27] A mixture of nitroglycerine and black powder, dynamite was developed as an industrial explosive, for mining and construction. However, the risks of premature explosion made it dangerous to use, and strict regulations and guidelines were established in every country where it was available.

Up to that time Fenians who had caused explosions, such as those in Manchester and Clerkenwell, London, in 1867, had used simple gunpowder. Johann Most, a German anarchist, saluted those Fenians, and spoke of 'the unquenchable spirit of destruction and annihilation which is the perpetual spring of new life'.[28] European and Russian anarchists seem to have been the first terrorists to use dynamite.

The two young emigrants had landed into Clan na Gael at a time of great difficulty, when the organisation was being pulled apart by the rivalry between Sullivan, an Irish-American who had little connection with Ireland, and Devoy. By 1881 Sullivan had become supreme 'boss', with Michael Boland and Denis Feeley, in a group known as the 'Triangle'. They advocated a terrorist policy of dynamiting buildings in Britain, and Dr Gallagher directed training on their behalf. Le Roux remarks disapprovingly that Sullivan was a bad judge of men, allowing himself to be conned by an English spy, Henri Le Caron, who headed the British intelligence network active among the Irish-American community.[29]

The idea of a dynamiting campaign was strongly supported by Jeremiah O'Donovan Rossa and Patrick Ford, editor of the *Irish World*. O'Donovan Rossa had been arrested after the 1863 Fenian uprising and sentenced to life imprisonment. An Amnesty Association, established in 1868 by IRB member John 'Amnesty' Nolan, was contacted by him through smuggled letters, and ran a campaign complaining about the harsh prison conditions suffered by IRB prisoners. O'Donovan Rossa was released in 1871, along with Devoy and others, on the condition of exile, and travelled with them to New York.

As irreconcilable as ever, O'Donovan Rossa began to raise money through Ford's *Irish World* for a dynamite campaign in England. He hoped this would cause enraged English citizens to attack Irish people living there, and therefore increase Irish support for separatism. John Devoy made an incendiary speech supporting the idea, but in fact Clan na Gael was opposed to it. They were planning a dynamite campaign of their own, but intended it to be much more organised and controlled than O'Donovan Rossa's 'one-man terrorist directorate'.[30] Devoy knew that the British population would be alienated from any sympathy for Ireland by such a campaign, and that it would encourage the British authorities to maintain a high alert in relation to Irish-American activities. This proved indeed to be the case.

O'Donovan Rossa broke with Clan na Gael in 1880, and between 1881 and 1883, under his direction, bombs were set off in Glasgow, Liverpool, London and Salford. There was one casualty, a young boy killed in Salford.[31] Devoy did not gain full control of Clan na Gael until 1890, by which time Tom Clarke was suffering his own consequences from the dynamite campaign.

In early 1883 Tom Clarke was about to become manager

of the Brighton Beach Hotel, near Coney Island. This was a large, well-known establishment, a centrepiece of the popular beach resort, so his employer must have been impressed by his capabilities. However, he was suddenly ordered by Timothy O'Riordan to leave his work and prepare for an early voyage. Aged 25, Clarke had been more than two years in New York, training with Dr Gallagher, and must have wondered if his chance to strike a blow for Ireland would ever come. The organisers of this expedition were Dr Gallagher himself and James Murphy (known as Albert Whitehead), who were going to England to supervise it. All of their activities were being observed by Le Caron's intelligence network, and information was passed back to Britain about them. Billy Kelly only heard of this journey when he received Clarke's trunk, with a note warning him not to tell Tom's family.

Clarke travelled separately from the others, via Boston, on a vessel which struck an iceberg. Rescued by a passing ship, he was landed in Newfoundland. He gave his name as 'Henry Hammond Wilson', and said he was an Englishman going home. He was given new clothes, and five pounds.[32] Because of the shipwreck, the spies who had been following him lost track of him, and he was able to land at Liverpool quite unobserved. He headed to London, and made contact with Gallagher and Whitehead. These were already being followed by British police agents, so Clarke again became an object of suspicion.[33]

The British police were at this stage developing from the early Bow Street Runners, and Robert Peel's 'Peelers' or 'bobbies' of the 1830s, into a more organised and professional force, with a detective section. At least thirty men were responsible for preventing political crime in London, although they complained that their resources were inadequate, against the money their enemies could deploy. As Le Caron later wrote, 'If plots are to be discovered in time … they can only be discovered through information coming from those associated with them. As I have shown, the men engaged in them are very highly paid. If it is to be made worth their while to speak, then the price offered by the British Government must be higher than that of the other paymasters'.[34]

These detectives intercepted mail, deciphered codes, and followed anyone who attracted suspicion. They also made use of informers; one of the men who had travelled with Gallagher and Whitehead, calling himself William Norman, was subsequently revealed to be an ex-Clan na Gael member, Joseph Lynch, when he turned state's evidence at their trials. One commentator remarked that it was 'astonishing to find what an amount of folly or vanity existed among these conspirators … the police everywhere were on the watch'.[35]

On 31 March 1883, Clarke rented a room at 17 Nelson Square, Blackfriars Road, London, telling the landlady he was a student. Whitehead was now in Birmingham, and had set up as a paint and colour merchant. Here he had a nitro-glycerine factory in his basement, and Clarke needed supplies. He wrote to Whitehead on 2 April, saying, 'Dear friend, If you are not otherwise engaged I would like the pleasure of your company at one of the theatres this evening. I will be at the place decided upon to meet on any such occasion at 6.30. Wilson'. This letter, like every other communication he sent while he was in England, was intercepted and read by the police.

Clarke's landlady gave evidence at his trial that he had not slept at his lodgings on the night of 3 April, and a 'Boots' of the Midland Hotel, Birmingham, stated that 'Wilson', having spent the night there, left hurriedly on the morning of 4 April. He had been to Whitehead's shop and collected several pounds of nitroglycerine.

The dynamiters were very casual in how they moved this dangerous liquid around. Pounds of it were carried in rubber containers – bags, waders, shooting-stockings. At his trial, part of the evidence against 'Wilson' was his purchase in Cheapside of two india-rubber bags: 'we do not often sell two at a time', remarked the salesman.[36] The weight of his portmanteau had also attracted attention from one of the railway porters. Clarke had 'feared that rough handling at the [railway] station, where the portmanteau had to be slid down a sliding board, might detonate them, and send station, porters, police and conspirators sky high. All went well, however…'[37]

A Birmingham police sergeant called into Whitehead's shop on 3 April pretending to be a painter, and noted that the owner's fingers 'were stained as if with acid'. That night police, using skeleton keys, entered the shop, searched the basement and found the evidence they were looking for. Whitehead was arrested the following morning. Detective-Inspector Littlechild, in overall charge of the operation, knew that 'Wilson' was due to meet Gallagher in London that day, and arrested both of them together. The incriminating portmanteau, full of dynamite, was sent to Woolwich Arsenal for examination. The eventual quantity of nitroglycerine discovered by the police was, according to experts, enough to blow up 'every street and house in London, from one end to the other'.[38] Gallagher was found to have £1,400 on his person.[39]

This did not mean the end of the dynamite campaign. In late 1883 and early 1884, two explosions took place in Glasgow, and several more in London. There was no further attempt to manufacture the explosive in England; it was brought from the USA, in slabs of what was called 'Atlas powder'.[40] In response to these attacks, the Special (Irish) Branch was set up at Scotland Yard, under renowned Chief Inspector 'Dolly' Williamson. An attempt to blow up London Bridge failed to destroy it, but the dynamiters involved, William Mackey Lomasney and John Fleming, disappeared, and seem to have been blown up by their own bomb.[41]

John Daly, another dynamite conspirator and the man who had sworn Clarke into the IRB, arrived in England from New York in October 1883. He stayed in London at the home of a collaborator, James Egan. Although the police followed him everywhere, he managed to evade them for one trip to Liverpool in April 1884, and was arrested at Birkenhead station on his return, with his coat-pockets apparently bulging with explosive devices. His niece Madge later wrote, '[Daly] got an urgent message from Dan O'Neill in Birkenhead, who said his son-in-law had brought explosives from the US, and he did not know what to do. He asked Uncle John to take the stuff and destroy it. Uncle John agreed, although he had never handled explosives before. When he reached the station, he was arrested. He knew O'Neill had sold him'.[42]

The campaign continued; on 30 May 1884, several bombs exploded in London, one, embarrassingly enough, beneath the offices of the Special (Irish) Branch. Fortunately, no-one was killed.

An interview with an anonymous source about the origins and development of Clan na Gael, published in the *Brooklyn Eagle* in 1883, asserts that Clan na Gael were pushed into dynamite activities by the more revolutionary members. 'They were novices in the business and not trained revolutionists like the [earlier] Fenians. Hence their failure and the arrest of the men. Had they been revolutionists, Lynch would never have lived to testify in the dock … Clan na Gael is composed in the main of respectable businessmen whose training has been the very opposite of the kind of education which dynamite revolutionists should receive.'[43] A later interview, about the informer Lynch, implies that he was introduced to the others by John Devoy:'There is no doubt but that Devoy was badly sold, a fact which does not reflect very much credit on a man supposed to be a revolutionist.'[44]

All the Clan na Gael conspirators were tried under the Treason-Felony Act of 1848, which had been designed to reduce their status from 'traitors' to 'felons'. As O'Donovan Rossa complained bitterly, this linked them with 'the garroters and Sodomites of England'; they regarded themselves as political prisoners. Treating them as men of low character backfired, because they were regarded as heroes by much of Irish public opinion. The Amnesty Association earlier had fought for the release of all Fenian prisoners into exile, on the grounds that they had been cruelly treated, but this was unlikely to work again. The authorities were determined to prevent Fenians from claiming 'special treatment' again. The *Times* said of the Treason-Felony Act, on 15 June 1883, that it was intended 'to clear up uncertainties, and to substitute in certain instances a milder sentence for offenders who were deemed too contemptible to be executed'.[45]

Trial and Sentence

The trial of Clarke and five companions opened at the

Old Bailey, London, on 11 June 1883. His co-accused were Thomas Gallagher (33, physician), John Curtin (34, engineer), William Ansburgh (21, no occupation), Albert Whitehead (23, painter) and Bernard Gallagher (29, iron moulder). Clarke had obviously shaved some years off his age for his alias, and is listed as Henry Hammond Wilson (22, clerk).

The charges against them included 'conspiring ... maliciously to destroy and damage by nitroglycerine and other explosive substances, with intent and for the purpose of enabling others to commit certain felonies and also for a conspiracy to murder'. All the prisoners pleaded 'Not Guilty', and the trial concluded on 14 June. It is worth noting, in the era of Guantanamo Bay, that although the public outcry was to lock them up and throw away the key, these terrorist suspects were allowed the full protection of British law. They could make their own statements from the dock, and these were reported at length in the newspapers; they were also provided with legal aid if they requested it.

Tom Clarke, or 'Henry Hammond Wilson', was one who chose to conduct his own defence. He felt he had as good a chance on his own as the others had, even with their British lawyers. He was right in that; the verdicts were never in doubt. He defended himself on the grounds that he had not actually committed any act as alleged, that he had not been proven to have committed such acts, and that intention to commit a crime did not in itself constitute a crime.

He acquitted himself reasonably well, considering his youth. Under cross-examination, Lynch, the informer, had to admit that he had not seen Clarke before. However, according to Le Roux, Clarke made an important mistake: 'Counsel was telling the Court that the explosive was made of certain elements when "Wilson", in a moment's absent-mindedness, hastened to correct him. "So", said Counsel, "you know all about it." The lesson made such an impression on him that he never again in his life said a word too much about anything…'

Clarke was offered the opportunity to address the jury on his own behalf, but said he would let the case go to them as it stood. 'The judge complimented him on his defence, adding that it was a pity such ability was misused.' Intriguingly, an unidentified correspondent writing to Louis Le Roux about his later biography of Clarke complains: 'There is no reference in the book to the coloured Barrister whose presence and friendliness made such an impression on Clarke at his trial, and who by smiles and frowns guided him in his questions and statements'.[46]

Two of the men, Ansburgh and Bernard Gallagher, were acquitted, but Patrick Gallagher, Whitehead, 'Wilson' and Curtin were sentenced to penal servitude for life (which meant at least twenty years). Press comment noted that the evidence against 'Wilson' and one of the others was not very complete, 'but their conduct … was not easily explicable on any hypothesis of innocence'. When sentence was passed, Clarke rose to address the court, but was hauled from the dock before he could say anything. On his way down, he was heard to say, 'Good-bye! We shall meet in heaven'.[47]

Chapter Two

Prisoner Number J464
1883-98

The nineteenth-century British prison system was a work in progress. Medieval-style punishments such as stocks and public whippings had long been discontinued, and public executions had ceased as the public developed a horror of the gruesome scenes. Between 1650 and 1750, laws known as the 'Bloody Code' had almost trebled the number of crimes for which people were executed, and the incessant use of capital punishment for relatively minor crimes such as theft gradually shifted public sympathy to the side of the executed criminal.

Prisons as we might understand them began to develop in the late eighteenth century, and the Penitentiary Act was passed in 1778. As the name implies, 'penance' was the primary aim. A petty criminal, such as a thief, would be put out of society's way for a time, and some kind of rehabilitation would be attempted. However, funding was not provided for the operation of this reforming act. Meanwhile local authorities developed their own prisons, for local petty crimes; they were not well funded, nor the warders well paid, and a prisoner's standard of living could depend entirely on bribing warders, either in cash or in kind – prostitution was often par for the course for female prisoners.

Because eighteenth-century Britain could remove criminals to its American colonies, transportation was seen as a cheap and painless option for serious crimes against the person or the state. However, after the American Revolution, British prisoners could no longer be sent across the Atlantic. For a time Australia was used as a substitute, but as proper administration was gradually established there, the colony objected to being used as a dumping-ground for criminals, and the system ceased. Besides, transportation was seen by reformers as a very arbitrary punishment. There was no way of finding out what happened to prisoners once they had left British shores – they might prosper, or return to crime, or they might die miserably. How could you ensure rehabilitation, if you did not keep prisoners where you could control them?

Now the British authorities were faced with a severe problem. Was there some way you could release prisoners and guarantee that they would not reoffend? Was rehabilitation possible? And how costly would such a system be? In 1810, a House of Commons select committee was appointed to look into the matter, and various approaches were tried.

Between 1815 and 1865, the emphasis was on attempts to reform prisoners. However, a spate of crimes by released prisoners frightened public opinion; the system was accused of being too soft, and it was insisted that prisons should be places of severe punishment first and rehabilitation second. Tom Clarke and his companions landed in prison just when this system of deterrence was fully established, between 1865 and 1895, and suffered the full force of it.[1]

At this time, religion was the determining factor when it came to the rule of law. British administrators during the Great Famine had believed in 'providentialism', that is, that God was punishing the Irish for their rebellious tendencies. This is one reason why relief was slow in coming, and grudging when it did come; one ought not to go against the will of God. In the same way, the developing prison system sought to save the sinner – indeed, the soul was seen as far more important than the body. Religious reformers argued that criminals had a capacity for remorse, 'which could be awakened by carefully legitimated and scientifically inflicted pain'.[2] The system was also influenced by the Rationalist school of thought, represented by Jeremy Bentham, a prison reformer: if people could be taught to reason correctly, they would not commit any more crimes.

At a later date, Charles Darwin's work on inherited

characteristics (*Origin of the Species*, 1859) and Francis Gal-
ton's work in the same area (*Hereditary Genius*, 1869; *Inquiry
into Human Faculty*, 1884) helped to encourage the theory
that many characteristics, such as criminal tendencies, are
inherited. This 'Social Darwinism' seemed to imply that there
was not much point in trying to reform criminals. Pseudo-
sciences such as phrenology attempted to prove criminal
tendencies by examining someone's head, or the shape of
their face.

In the 1830s a commissioner was sent to the USA to study
two systems there, the 'separate' and the 'silent'. The 'separate'
system operated on the principle of 'moral contagion', sepa-
rating prisoners from one another. They could communicate
only with prison staff, work in their cells, take part in religious services and education, and have a daily hour of exercise in the open air. Conversations during exercise could be
'a great medium of evil communications', according to Sir
Edmund Du Cane, Chair of the Directorate of Convict Prisoners, so each prisoner exercised in solitude. 'First offenders'
were kept apart from recidivists.

It was carefully worked out that nine months was the maximum time for which the 'separate' system could be enforced;
if the prisoner was kept in isolation for longer than that, there
was a strong risk that insanity would result. It was tested in
Pentonville in 1842, for a period of eighteen months, and
Du Cane admitted that 'the minds of the prisoners became

enfeebled by long-continued isolation.'[3] However, the Reverend D. Nihill, who presided over this system at Millbank Prison, argued that morals were no less a consideration than health.[4] Another complaint against this system was that a person's social qualities were repressed, rather than encouraged; those who experienced it would hardly be able to fit in with ordinary society on release. Modern thought reckons that about nine *days* is as long as someone can suffer complete isolation without consequences.

The second system allowed prisoners to work in association, but in silence, so they could not conspire together. This 'silent' system was criticised because the total lack of communication was so unnatural. Prisoners would not be able to resist the temptation to communicate in whatever way possible, and would then have to be punished. This was surely unfair. The 'silent' system also depended to a great extent on the quality of the staff; they would need to be well trained. Ultimately, it was decided to combine the two systems; a period of 'separation' would come first, as a preparation for association with other prisoners, and then the 'silent' system would begin operation. Prisons were nationalised in 1877, and the penal system was encouraged towards uniformity.

The silence and isolation were designed to throw the prisoner's mind in upon itself. Du Cane wrote that the prisoner 'cannot fail to feel that, however agreeable may have been his previous life, probably one of idleness and excitement, he pays dearly for it by the dull monotony, hard work, a diet which is sufficient, but no more than sufficient, and deprived of every luxury he has been accustomed to indulge in, and above all, by the absence of freedom, and the constant supervision'. Such a prisoner is 'likely to feel sorry, and welcome advice about avoiding evil in future'.

'Above all things,' affirms Du Cane, 'it is necessary that the prisoner should feel that the rules are carried out justly and fairly, that the officers are simply administering the law, and that in case of any abuse of power on the part of an officer, he will be held answerable for it ... Every prisoner has the right of appeal against the act of those above him.'

The system strikes us now with its severity, and its utter incomprehension of the psychological effects of isolation, but that was not understood then – Sigmund Freud's work on psychoanalysis did not begin to appear till the 1890s. Even at the time, however, there were voices to say that such treatment placed an inhuman strain on a man or woman.

The writer Charles Dickens was not, he insisted, a maudlin sympathiser with notorious criminals, nor a believer in 'those good old customs of the good old times which made England...in respect of her criminal code and her prison regulations, one of the most bloody-minded and barbarous countries on the earth'. However, when he visited a Philadelphia prison which operated on a system of 'rigid, strict, and hopeless solitary confinement', he decided that it was cruel and wrong in its effects: 'I hold this slow and daily tampering with the mysteries of the brain, to be immeasurably worse than any torture of the body: and because its ghastly signs and tokens are not so palpable to the eye and sense of touch as scars upon the flesh ... I the more denounce it.' This prison was an extreme example, in which prisoners never moved out of their cells, even for exercise, and had no contact with the outside world, but he accepted that even a brief experience of solitary confinement would have a damaging effect.[5]

Prison diet was kept at a fairly low level, just enough to keep a prisoner healthy and to prevent scurvy; to offer an improved diet as a reward for good behaviour would 'appeal to baser feelings'. More importantly, there was a lot of economic depression during the later nineteenth century in urban Britain. It would have aroused public feeling if prisoners could be shown to have a better diet than free, working men. Luxuries such as beer and tea were forbidden. Punishment for minor offences consisted of a certain number of days on bread and water.

Good behaviour could earn a prisoner more letters and visits, and a system of marks awarded for good work would earn a gratuity, payable at the end of the sentence. The marks were recorded on a card, so the prisoner could check his own progress, and be encouraged to improve, and learn habits of discipline. The work provided was not necessarily designed to teach the prisoner a useful trade; much of it was described by a prison official as 'incessant, often arduous and painfully harassing'. The health of many prisoners was permanently damaged by 'hard labour', which was not defined in law.

Immediately their trial ended, Clarke and his companions were taken to Millbank Prison, where 'Henry Hammond Wilson' became prisoner number J464. The surveillance of the 'silent system' there was very close, but the prisoners were able to communicate with one another. They dug out a bit of the lead pivot of a cell door, with which they could write on the bits of toilet paper provided. Writing of Millbank, Tom remembered 'a dreary time of solitary confinement… with a short daily exercise varying the monotony. Day after day all alike, no change, maddening silence…'[6] However, they were treated just the same as ordinary prisoners, which he later appreciated.

They remained in Millbank until August, when they were removed to Chatham Prison in Kent, where a special wing had been reserved for them. Chatham was noted in the British penal system for having the toughest system of all, and it was felt that these notorious Irish dynamiters would need not only to be prevented at all costs from escaping, and from communicating with outside supporters, but would also have to be protected from other prisoners. Received at Chatham on 25 August 1883, aged 25 years (but listed as being 22),

Tom Clarke was described as being 5 ft 8 ins in height, and weighing 133 lbs.

Letters and visitors were strictly regulated. Letters were of course censored before being sent on, and any 'political' material was removed; this was also done with letters received from outside. Sometimes a letter would be copied to give to the prisoner, with the offending material left out, and these copied letters are still in the files. An official letter to Clarke's brother Alf, in 1896, indicated that of the seven letters forwarded to Tom, he had been allowed to choose one, and the other six were being returned.[7]

One visitor was allowed every six months, but if a prisoner broke any regulation his visiting privileges were withdrawn, and he had to wait a further six months. This was naturally very hard on him, but was equally hard on family members who had perhaps looked forward to this visit for months, making preparations for the long journey from Ireland. During the third year of imprisonment, a visitor would be allowed every four months, and from the fourth year, every three months. Visits were not limited to relatives only. For example, John Redmond, an Irish Parliamentary Party MP, visited Tom Clarke and others several times, but these visits were to provide legal advice, and were not at the expense of family members. Redmond was very active in the amnesty movement, and made several speeches in the House of Commons on behalf of the prisoners.

Right: Tom Clarke as a
young man.
Below: Kathleen Daly in
1901, before her marriage.

IRISH
NATIONAL AMNESTY ASSOCIATION

ROUND ROOM, ROTUNDA

A GREAT

DEMONSTRATION

WILL BE HELD ON

FRIDAY EVG., OCTOBER 21

To Welcome the Recently

RELEASED POLITICAL PRISONERS

The victims of the infamous Spy and Informer, NED JIM McDERMOTT, after their Fifteen years cruel imprisonment in English jails,

MESSRS. WILSON, DALTON & FEATHERSTON

Who will leave the Committee Rooms, 41 York St. on that Evening at 7.30, o'clock accompanied by the

CITY BANDS!

And National Bodies, with Torches, and preceded by Stephen's Green, Grafton Street, Westmoreland Street, and O'Connell Street, to the

ROUND ROOM, ROTUNDA

WHEN A GREAT

PUBLIC MEETING

WILL BE HELD AT 8.30 P.M. AT WHICH

MR. MICHAEL LAMBERT

(PRESIDENT OF THE ASSOCIATION)

MAUD GONNE | JAMES F. EGAN

MR. J. E. REDMOND, MP.

SEVERAL IRISH MEMBERS OF PARLIAMENT
MEMBERS OF THE DUBLIN CORPORATION

Of the VARIOUS NATIONAL and TRADE SOCIETIES and OTHER DISTINGUISHED
CITIZENS AND FRIENDS OF THE AMNESTY CAUSE THROUGH IRELAND

ADMISSION FREE!

The Balcony will be Reserved, Tickets, for which can be obtained from any of the Members
of the Committee, or at the Committee Rooms, 41 York Street.

GOD SAVE IRELAND

CORRIGAN & WILSON, Printers, Dublin.

Right: John Daly.
Below: Tom and Kathleen Clarke, around the time of their marriage.
Opposite: Amnesty International poster celebrating the release of 'Wilson' (Tom Clarke) and other Fenian prisoners.

Above: Tom Clarke's sister Hannah and their mother, Mary Clarke.

Right: Tom Clarke outside his shop, 75A Parnell Street, probably 1909, with business card superimposed.
Below: Advertisement for John Daly's bakery in Limerick.

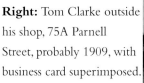

THOMAS J. CLARKE.

10 RICHMOND AVENUE, DUBLIN.

8 HOWARD STREET, BELFAST.

JOHN DALY'S
BAKERIES,
26 WILLIAM STREET
AND
SARSFIELD STREET,
LIMERICK.

All Classes of Feeding Stuffs Stocked.

Above: Tom and Kathleen's eldest son, John Daly, known as 'Daly'.

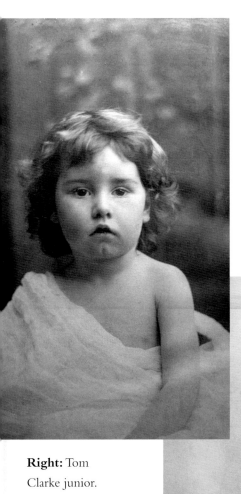

Left: Emmet Clarke as a baby.

Right: Tom Clarke junior.

Above: Crowds on their way to the O'Donovan Rossa funeral, August 1915.
Right: Receipt relating to the O'Donovan Rossa Funeral Fund, on Clarke's shop notepaper.

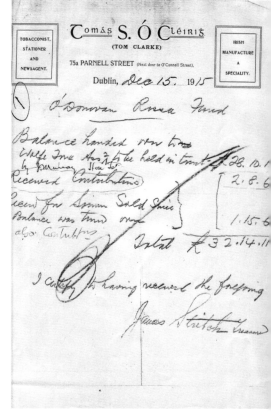

Because Tom Clarke had been tried as 'Henry Hammond Wilson', this remained his name for the next fifteen years. It was unknown to his family and friends, and it was nine months before they became aware of it. His first visitor was his old friend from Dungannon and New York, Billy Kelly, who had seen and recognised Clarke's photograph in the newspapers. Billy had returned to Ireland in 1883, and kept in touch with Clarke's sister Hannah, sending Tom's trunk back to her. He also visited Clarke's sister Maria, then living in Clonakilty, County Cork.[8] Kelly posed as a relative in order to make the prison visit.

Clarke had to wait another eighteen months for another visit, also from Kelly, and he was almost six years in prison before a member of his family was enabled to visit him, on 5 February 1889. This was his sister Hannah, who had not seen him for nine years; she visited him again on 1 August[9.] It was probably lack of money that prevented his sister from making the long journey by boat and train from Dublin more often, and Clarke may have lost some scheduled visits by breaking the regulations.

In early 1884 Clarke recognised two new prisoners, John Daly, K562, who had sworn him into the IRB in Dungannon, and James Egan, K561, who had been arrested and tried with Daly. Daly had been sentenced to penal servitude for life, and Egan for twenty years. These three became close friends over the dreadful years ahead, and developed many ingenious ways of circumventing the tight regulations on communication.

The 'silent' system came very hard on the prisoners, with its complete ban on the most trivial of chat, or even the exchange of a wink. Gradually several of the Fenian prisoners, notably Gallagher and Whitehead, began to show signs of mental derangement, but this was denied by the prison authorities. Clarke states that he and others did all they could to draw attention to this, but that Governor Harris would not listen to them, and any letters mentioning it were censored or suppressed. Tom quotes a letter he wrote to Redmond in 1895, which of course never got to its recipient, in which he described Whitehead eating crushed glass in the carpenter's shop. He was able to put the facts before Redmond when the latter visited him, and shortly afterwards Gallagher and Whitehead were released, along with several others.[10] Both men were later certified insane.

Only the sternest mental discipline enabled prisoners to live through these conditions, and to reach the end of their imprisonment with their minds more or less intact. Daly, a gregarious man who loved to talk, dealt with the situation by making continual complaints. Each complaint generated a new file and a range of interviews with chaplains, doctors and/or the Governor himself. Daly's dossier is by far the thickest among the prison records, and he had clearly decided that it was worth the few days' punishment to get the opportunity to leave his cell and talk to someone, anyone, face to face. He must have realised that utter silence and separation would cause him to descend into madness if he did not fight it.

Ordinary punishment, for minor offences, consisted of a certain number of days in solitary confinement, on a diet of bread and water. Daly was very careful not to cross the line which led to physical punishment. Such behaviour included shouting, attacking another prisoner or a staff member, or threatening suicide or self-harm. For any of these, a prisoner could be given 36 lashes of the whip or 28 strokes of the birch. Men who risked receiving such punishments had clearly broken down and lost all control; Daly never did so. It must be admitted that the prison stuck rigidly to its own rules; the temptation to teach Daly a lesson for being a nuisance must have been severe, but he was never beaten, because he never broke any of the relevant regulations.

Tom Clarke dealt with the privations quite differently. He did make some complaints to the prison authorities in the early years, but soon decided that there was little point – nothing was ever going to improve. Instead, he went into his own head, making mathematical calculations with a slate and pencil, or substitutes for them. According to his memoir, he counted bricks and bolts in his cell, calculating the weight of the bricks and the number used in building the entire prison; he calculated the number of buttons on the clothing of the whole population of the prison; he measured clippings from his weekly haircut, and estimated that six feet of hair had been cut over thirteen years.[11]

A constant source of stress was the miserable reading allowance. Prisoners were allowed two books per year, and distribution was fairly random. Clarke complained that he was often given silly fiction, or children's books. However he was once given a copy of *Cassell's Popular Educator*. This contained lessons in shorthand, and he taught himself this skill, eventually translating the whole Bible into shorthand (twice), when he was given a copy. The light in the cells was poor, and he complained later that his sight had been permanently weakened by trying to read without proper light – later photographs never show him without spectacles. Further stress was caused by the constant checking every night; the slamming of the hatch rendered normal sleep impossible: 'With the same loud noise the trap would be banged all through the night at hour intervals. The prisoner might get a few short snatches of sleep between the inspections…'[12]

Clarke's memoir complained of the 'Special Search', which happened about twice a month – 'strip-searching', during which every orifice was explored with a torch 'to such a disgustingly indecent extent that I must not here do more than imply the nature of it'. This would be accompanied by 'a running fire of comments'. At least four times a day, prisoners received a 'rub-down' search, when they were 'mauled' all over. Once a week their hair was cut, with scissors, each prisoner cutting another's hair; when Clarke had his ear cut by a ham-handed fellow-prisoner, the latter was admonished by the warder for 'damaging Government property' (possibly in jest). Clippers were later substituted, thus avoiding the 'regular ridges of cuts…where the skin had been clipped away'.[13]

Communication was the most important element in holding on to sanity. When imprisoned with his brother after the 1867 Fenian rising, Daly had learnt a form of Morse code, and did his best to pass this on to other prisoners. They had each been given a slate and pencil to communicate with the warders, and Daly was discovered putting the code on the back of his slate and passing it to another prisoner. Daly, Clarke and several others had their slates confiscated, and had to do without them for the remainder of their terms. This meant they had to ask the prison chaplain for the library books they wanted; they were not allowed to talk to anyone else, and could no longer write.

They developed a system of tapping on their tin plates, and on the walls of their cells, passing news from one to another. This was noticed, and a warder who was an ex-sailor and knew Morse code was moved to their section. He was able to confirm that messages were being passed, though some of the code was in Irish, and he could not decipher it. Both Daly and Clarke suffered punishments over the years for being caught passing messages, but despite this they kept up a lively correspondence. Once, Clarke even managed to contrive a couple of pages of a 'newspaper', on tissue paper – he was working as a stereotyper in the printers' shop at the time. He managed to pass it to Daly, who was highly entertained. He recalls that never a week passed without at least one note from Daly or Egan, whatever the difficulties. 'Tell that to the prison authorities and they would say it was utterly impossible. But we, too, had reduced our business to a scientific system – it was diamond cut diamond.'[14]

The constant complaints of the Irish prisoners, and the intense and passionate campaign organised by the Amnesty Association in Britain and Ireland, eventually led to the Chatham Enquiry of 1890, an official parliamentary enquiry. The main complainants were Daly, who wrote 30 pages of complaint, Egan (10 pages) and Clarke (14 pages). They mentioned the restricted amount of exercise they received, in a small dark yard; the use of cold baths; the inadequacy of the toilet-paper issue (it was pointed out that if they did not use it for messaging, the supply would be adequate); careless medical treatment (Daly was once given castor oil by mistake, and, more seriously, an overdose of belladonna which affected him badly); and a prevailing sense that the warders were prejudiced against them, as Irish dynamiters, and treated them more roughly than prisoners in other sections.

The final report rejected most of the complaints but did

agree that the practice of making prisoners sit in their cells on a fixed log, instead of a movable stool, should be discontinued. [15] The inspectors also commented on the treatment of sick prisoners in their cells, not the infirmary, which Clarke had particularly complained about, as it meant that sick men got no rest because of the constant activity of the prison. The report recommended that warders should be requested to be quieter if a prisoner was ill.

The prisoners complained of deliberately brutal or inconsiderate treatment by warders, such as throwing food, bumping into prisoners with intent to injure, or using foul and insulting language. However, the inspectors found '...that no organised system of ill-treatment has been pursued... [apart from] the misconduct of individual officers, such as must from time to time occur among a large staff of men drawn from the class from which subordinate prison officers are selected'.

The inspectors added, 'We have no doubt that the prisoners generally, and especially those who have had more education than the others, find the restraints and discipline of prison life to be irksome'. However, they did not find 'anything in the general or medical treatment of any of the prisoners which would lead us to suggest that any of them should be removed'.

It was clearly felt that these men were 'first offenders', many of them with a decent level of education, so they would naturally be greatly affected by their circumstances. This view was spelt out by one of the chaplains, the Rev William Alton:

'Q: What do you feel in regard to the prisoner Wilson [Clarke]?

'A: I think he feels it very much…those are a different class to the others, and naturally they would feel their imprisonment more.

'Q: Should they not have thought of that before they committed their offences?

'A: I do not mean to express any sympathy with them… but as their priest I thought it my duty to express my view as to their mental condition…their sentences are longer, and they have not been in prison before, and they feel it more acutely.'[16]

Clarke's total career in Chatham can be summed up very briefly through the basic lists of work, visitors and punishments, but these take no account of the main effects of the imprisonment, the constant stress of silence and lack of human contact. He worked as a cleaner until 1886; an iron-moulder until 1889; a darner till 1889, and then as a printer until he left Chatham. His medical records list a burn on his foot in 1888, as well as bouts of palpitations and influenza. He was diagnosed as having a 'systolic bruit' (a heart murmur), but it was not thought to be serious. It may have been the result of his years of heavy labour in the iron-foundry. He received fourteen separate punishments over the years, mainly for trying to communicate with other prisoners; he did once strike another prisoner, but since he only received two days' punishment, it must not have been considered a severe offence. The heaviest punishment he received, of 23 days' bread and water and the loss of 360 marks (which contributed to the money he earned in prison), was for having a piece of newspaper in his possession. He later insisted that he had known nothing about it; it was found in the corridor on the way to the chapel, and he was accused of having dropped it. John Daly, speaking later of this long punishment, saw Tom come out at the end of the 23 days: 'when he was set into the ring [for exercise] he marched around the ring with us. His eye was bright although he tottered and fell. Deep down in my heart I declared that day if Ireland had 1,000 men like "Henry Hammond Wilson", England's power might look to itself'.[17] Tom himself commented, 'I have been forced to chew the rags I got to clean my tinware to try and allay the hunger pangs'.[18]

In February 1889 he was visited by Chief Inspector Littlechild, who had arrested him.

This visit by Littlechild to 'Wilson' and seven other Irish prisoners was to try to get them to go before the Parnell Commission, which was investigating accusations against Charles Stewart Parnell; he hoped to implicate the Irish Party leader in the dynamite activities. Clarke flatly refused to be used for this purpose, although he was offered early release and a civil service job: 'If a single word of information would get me out of here tomorrow, sooner than give it to you, I'd prefer to remain here till the day of judgment. Please take that as final'.[19]

In the Home Office, opinion was growing that it might be as well to remove the Irish prisoners to a different prison. They would obviously never settle in Chatham, and the Secretary of State considered that 'it might not be unwise to remove Daly and Egan to some other prison, where the means of safe custody equally exist. Public opinion would be satisfied by such a step'. Du Cane was strongly against this move, arguing that these 'most difficult prisoners have been well managed at Chatham and with all their ingenuity, unscrupulousness and their irritability they have not been able to substantiate any grievance, nor have they been able to carry on surreptitious communication with their friends outside...It is most probably their failure to find a treacherous assistant among the Staff at Chatham which prompts them and their friends to press for a removal elsewhere...'[20]

However, political factors indicated a change in policy. Consequently, the Fenian prisoners were moved to Portland Prison in 1891, which had a slightly easier regime. Tom Clarke, now aged 33, arrived there on 19 January 1891, and John Daly on 23 January.

In Portland, Clarke worked as a tailor and shoemaker,

and lastly entered the smith's shop. Here, Clarke was finally able to make contact with someone on the outside. He was packing tinware in crates to be sent to Woolwich Arsenal, and managed to smuggle in a request for newspapers. To his delight, a large number of papers arrived in the next batch of crates, and he was able to move them by degrees to his cell, and on to the other prisoners. It is difficult to imagine such a success in Chatham.

In December 1891, a petition was organised on behalf of Tom Clarke by neighbours and friends in Dungannon, County Tyrone. The petition argued that he had been little more than a boy at the time, and under bad influences; that he had been assured that only buildings would be targeted, with no loss of life; that he had now served over eight years; that his father had been a loyal servant of the Crown, and his brother Alfred, aged 21, was then serving in the Royal Artillery. The petition was organised by T. O'Neill Russell, MP for South Tyrone, and collected signatures from public figures such as magistrates, town commissioners, poor law guardians and clergy, as well as three officers from James Clarke's regiment, the Mid Ulster Artillery. Many of the signatories were Protestant.[21]

The petition was presented to Queen Victoria in early 1892, but had no effect. Louis Le Roux confidently asserts that Clarke was not aware of the terms of the petition, but if he had been, 'he would have torn it in pieces sooner than allow it to go forward on his behalf'.[22] He was not going to apologise for anything he had done.

John Daly was released, after a vigorous Amnesty Association campaign, in 1896. A letter to Louis Le Roux, about a draft of his biography of Clarke, throws an interesting light on the two friends at this time: 'The Prison Chapter contains no reference to the question of religion or to the difference arising out of the question of religion which so estranged the two prisoners that they did not avail of the opportunities which they still had to communicate with each other during the last six or nine months that Daly was in jail'.[23] This would be very sad, if true. It is surely unlikely that religion would be a matter of contention between Clarke and Daly; neither man ever seemed to be particularly religious, and both were alienated from the Catholic Church by its excommunication of the Fenians.

Whether the alleged rupture is true or not, it is unarguable that the hardest time of all that Clarke spent in prison was between Daly's release in 1896 and his own in late 1898. He was completely isolated; almost all the other Fenians had either died or been released, and the only other one left, Henry Burton, remained permanently in the infirmary. Companionship had been the only thing which had made the imprisonment half-way bearable; now all that had been lost. He describes himself as being 'bird alone': 'It was then "strict silence" to the letter…but the usual routine of prison life went on…; the escort marching me off and reporting to each superior office he passed what his "party" consisted of. "One man, sir"…after work to be searched again, after which to be … marched back to my cells for meals or for bed, and all this carried on without a detail of prison ceremonial omitted.' Visiting him in December 1896, his sister Hannah wrote of her grief and shock at how much he had changed since her last visit: 'He is now little short of being a complete wreck – pale, emaciated, and generally broken down…Of late his health has almost entirely failed him.' He was suffering more palpitations and dizziness.[24]

Hannah had her own problems too. In July 1897, John Daly wrote to her (addressing her as Dora, her family's pet name) about her mother's financial worries; they were under threat of eviction from their home. He was critical of the Dublin branch of the Amnesty Association for failing to help the family of an imprisoned Fenian, and wrote to a member of the committee, '… I am inclined to think, that Clark[e] would not be either pleased or thankful for a visit from the Association that could not afford to help his mother out of the difficulty she finds herself in now'. Daly guaranteed Hannah that the money would be forthcoming, either from the Association or from himself, to enable Mrs Clarke to buy a small house where she could take in boarders.[25]

By 1898, Tom Clarke had completed fifteen years of his sentence, and the Irish clamour for his release grew. In June, Redmond was informed by the authorities that Clarke's sentence would now be treated as one of twenty years, rather than life, and he could be released with five years remitted for good behaviour. It was settled that he would be released 'on licence' (bound by some restrictions) on 14 September 1898.[26]

In his prison memoir, Clarke lists his Golden Rules for the long-sentence prisoner:

'Clinch your teeth hard and never say die.

'Keep your thoughts off yourself all you can.

'No mooning or brown studies.

'Guard your self-respect (if you lost that you'd lose the backbone of your manhood).

'Keep your eyes wide open and don't bang your head against the wall.'

In the same memoir, he includes a detailed description of the effects of the 'silent system', and of solitary confinement. 'In the early years of his imprisonment, [a prisoner] may be safe enough while his memory furnishes him with subject after subject to give the mind pleasurable occupation as he turns them over. In this way thoughts and ideas one after the other are turned over and examined until finally the whole stock has been under review. Commencing again, idea after idea is examined afresh, but with far less interest than the first time, if no new view-point can be found when dealing with a particular idea. On and on this goes until the end of the stock is reached again. Starting again, it is found that some of the ideas and memories have no further interest; the mind is sick of them; they have been turned over so much that they are too stale to arouse any further interest. Such as remain and still retain interest are once more reviewed and turned over. Finally there comes a time when by this process of elimination there remains not a single idea of the original stock that has not been quite "played out" and has now become hateful. The silent system then wins, for the mind, though more or less enfeebled by this time, must occupy itself with something, and the dreary wretchedness and misery of the convict prison that have been kept at arm's length during the struggle now get their innings, while the spectre of insanity hovers close by waiting to take charge and complete the work of the silent system.'[27]

The truth of the closing sentence is revealed in an undated handwritten list of the prisoners who shared these years with Clarke, Daly and Egan. Among those released in 1881 and 1883, McGrath is noted as 'dead', Gallagher 'health shattered and insane', Curtin 'health shattered', Whitehead 'insane', Deasy 'dead', Flanagan 'insane', McCullagh 'discharged because of ill health', McCabe 'insane, now dead', Devany 'discharged because of ill health, insane', Drumm, Kelly and Donnelly all dead, Casey 'insane'. Listed for 1884 are Burton, 'health shattered', Gilbert [Gillard?] 'discharged, health shattered', Harkness 'dead' and Duff 'insane'.[28]

It is no wonder that the man who eventually emerged from prison had a soul forged in steel and a heart that burned for vengeance.

Chapter Three

Freedom and Family
1898-1907

Tom Clarke emerged from the gates of Pentonville prison in London on Thursday 29 September, 1898, having been escorted there from Portland. An account in the *Irish Daily Independent* states that he was met at the prison gate by his brother Alfred and his close prison friend John Daly, and was brought to the home of a neighbour from the old days in Tyrone, Joseph Hart. That evening he was reunited with another prison comrade, James Egan.[1]

Kathleen Clarke's version is slightly different, asserting that John Daly had not known of Clarke's release in time to meet him.[2] Louis Le Roux's account differs again from both of these, stating that Tom was not met by his brother, although Alfred had been notified of the date of the release, and that he was instead greeted at the prison gate by both John Daly and James Egan before they accompanied him to Hart's home.[3] A letter from Mrs Hart to Tom's biographer, Le Roux, recalls

Daly and Egan calling for her husband, and the three of them escorting Tom back to her house. 'They brought him back to our place, had breakfast and spent the day with us, leaving in time for the night journey to Ireland. In my writing album they each wrote a few lines over their names; these we treasure with some souvenirs sent us by poor Tom...'[4]

However it fell out, Tom Clarke was at last free, and able to resume his own name. He arrived in Dublin on 8 October, and settled down with his mother and sister in Kilmainham. The *Independent* journalist describes Clarke as of medium height and intelligent aspect, but with face and body emaciated, and his shoulders stooped. For some months before his release, he said when interviewed, he had been allowed to work outside, so was brown from the sun, and had also been built up with daily doses of cod liver oil and malt. A later account describes him as 'so thin and spare that he looked as if every scrap of flesh and all material things were burnt away, as if only the vital spiritual forces of his personality remained. His face was refined, deeply marked with the lines of sufferings and endurance, yet humorous and kindly. His eyes were quick, alert, and his whole personality gave the impression of strength, decision and intelligence'.[5]

As John Daly had experienced on his own release, Clarke was much in demand for celebratory meetings and receptions, and was feted as a public martyr for Ireland. This must have been overwhelming after so many years surrounded by

silence, particularly for a man of retiring disposition. Gerard
Conlon of the Guildford Four, wrongly convicted almost a
hundred years later, expressed it well: 'I had gone away as a
kid ... I came out more mature, but I still wasn't sure whether
I could communicate with people in a meaningful way. I
needed time to work out where I was in this new world ...
I had to begin to make relationships with friends and family
that were fifteen years older than when I last saw them'.[6]
Tom Clarke came home to live with his mother and his sister
Hannah; he had not seen his mother since he had left Ireland
originally, but she rejoiced to meet him again, having given
him up for lost. His father had died four years earlier, on 18
March 1894, aged 64, of pneumonia. The world he came out
to was also new and bewildering; for example, horses were
being rapidly superseded by bicycles and automobiles.

Dungannon provided one of the largest public receptions
in October; its nationalists welcomed home their heroic son
with open arms. Here he gave his first ever public speech,
expressing his gratitude for all the support he had received,
condemning the way in which he had been treated, and
crediting the strength of his resistance to British rule to his
knowledge of Irish history.[7] Another large reception took
place in Dublin on 23 November, hosted by the Ulster-
men's (Dublin) '98 Club. The year 1898 was, of course, the
centenary of the United Irishmen rebellion, and Clarke's
release proved a triumphant culmination for this year of

commemorations. Nationalist Ireland was on an upswing.

The most insistent calls for Clarke's presence came from his prison comrade John Daly. Now the first nationalist mayor of Limerick, through the newly-franchised working-class vote, Daly had started his term of office by removing the royal arms from Limerick's city hall, and the medallion he designed for his link in the mayoral chain portrayed two crossed pikes and a pair of handcuffs. He had taken a major part in events celebrating the 1798 rebellion, and the City Council agreed to his request to make Tom Clarke a Freeman of the City to mark that event. Clarke did not entirely welcome this public honour, as a letter from Daly dated 9 February 1899 urged him to overcome his 'natural modesty' and accept it.[8] Clarke finally travelled to Limerick to accept the Freedom of the City on 2 March 1899. Again he nerved himself to make a speech, dwelling on his friendship with John Daly, forged behind prison walls, and once more emphasising the importance of history in firing his enthusiasm for Ireland's cause.

It was natural that he should be invited to stay in Daly's home – a crowded household of Daly's mother, sister, widowed sister-in-law, eight nieces and one nephew, Edward.[9] Clarke was welcomed by all, of course, as John's close friend, but rapidly became popular in his own right, and blossomed under the attention of so many young women. Indeed, he revealed an unexpected taste for practical jokes and funning, and delighted in teasing the girls as they served in the shop linked with the bakery which John Daly had established. After so many years of deprivation, he appreciated good food, and had a particularly sweet tooth; he always wanted to know what was on the menu for 'the afterclap', as he called the dessert. Another aftermath of his prison days was an inability ever to feel fully warm, and he always wanted the fire built up. They also noted his difficulty at sitting with his knees under a table, after so many years using a fixed stool and fixed table.

One Daly niece in particular attracted his attention, and this was reciprocated. By the time he left Limerick – after a few weeks in this bustle of constant chat, music, card-games, laughter, noisy arguments, strong personalities and a menagerie of cats and dogs – Kathleen Daly, the third eldest, a blonde, blue-eyed girl with a lovely smile, had agreed to write to him. This was initially on behalf of her Uncle John, who always disliked 'slinging the ink', as he phrased it. In her own memoir, Kathleen admits that she was rather disappointed when she met Clarke first, as her uncle John had always portrayed his friend in heroic terms. Clarke, small, slight and weakened by imprisonment, with a hesitant manner, was hardly what they had all been expecting, but very shortly 'the man Uncle John had portrayed was revealed'.[10]

Their correspondence continued till the summer in a formal manner, Clarke signing himself 'Your very own friend,

Thomas J Clarke'. He mentions how much he had enjoyed himself with them: 'you can have no idea how delightfully pleasant my last visit …was – Indeed I didn't quite realize it myself till it drew to an end'. Kathleen deprecates her letter-writing skills, apologising for filling the pages with chat and gossip and nothing very important, but he insists, 'what you decry in your letters is the very thing that I would wish to see in them and begging your pardon – am I not the best judge?'[11]

Arriving back in Dublin, Clarke, still living in his mother's home and with little money, started looking for a job. He had earned £3 in all over his many years of labour in prison, but had staunchly refused to accept it when he was freed. He would not accept the clothes offered either, and Mrs Hart had had to bring him a suit and hat to wear on his release. All he took away from prison was his collection of old letters, which, he said, were very dear to him.[12] He kept in contact with many old friends in England, and visited there for some days in March 1899. He had written to the governor of Portland Prison in January, hoping to be allowed to visit Henry Burton, L262, the last Fenian prisoner left, but this was not permitted. Clarke says in this letter that none of Burton's family in the United States could visit him because of the cost, and that he knew himself from experience how much a friendly face could mean.[13]

In April he and his family played host to Burton on his

release from prison. Burton had been ill for a long time, and Clarke describes him to Kathleen as 'an extremely peculiar and eccentric fellow'. 'He sometimes forgets that I had ever been in prison and tells me some awful and marvellous things that had happened to him in prison. When he … piles on the agony I am simply reduced to a state of speechless astonishment at the terrible sufferings he has endured and the heroic bravery he displayed – Good Heavens but he is an awful fellow…'[14]

He was rebuilding his relations with his mother and sisters, aided by their mutual love of gardening, and interest in flowers: 'We here are all very fond of flowers and have now a great stock of almost everything in our little strip of farm-land in the back yard', he writes in May; in June he had a long country stroll with 'Dora' (Hannah), who had him 'pounding through old ditches and through hedges' to gather wild flowers; in August they visited a big Flower Show – 'we are all very fond of anything like that'.[15] Clarke had been uncertain of his mother's welcome, as she would not have approved of his revolutionary career, but she was obviously pleased to have him home. The Clarkes were not a demonstrative family, and were far more emotionally restrained than the Dalys.

Clarke was highly entertained by the elevation of his ex-convict friend John Daly, and mentions to Kathleen that he has heard quite a number of people 'speak in terms of praise and admiration of what John is doing since he became Mayor, and of the way he is doing the business, and I assure you it delights my heart to listen to it all'. And in June, after Daly had protested over the Loyal Toast at a dinner by singing a hymn, 'there is a comical side to that sure enough … It's a pity that sort of thing doesn't be published in the papers…'[16]

The Amnesty Association applied itself to finding a living for Tom Clarke, and in May 1899 he was assured that the position of clerk of Rathdown Poor Law Union, in County Wicklow, was his for the asking. His candidacy was supported by numerous public figures on the nationalist side, including the parish priest of Donaghmore, County Tyrone, who had known Tom as a young teacher in Dungannon. All the representations failed, however, and the job went elsewhere.[17]

Despite this disappointment, he had time to worry about Kathleen's health. The weather was extremely warm that spring, and he was concerned about her hours of work, running a dressmaking business with her sister Agnes: 'It is too bad that you and Agg are kept so busy that you can't at least have a few hours in the open air these beautiful evenings … success is a good thing worth working for but obtaining it at the price of one's health would be buying it too dearly … [your sisters] Madge and Eily [Eileen] must feel it unpleasantly warm in the shop. Theirs is even a worse case than your own long hours'.[18] Kathleen had trained with a Mrs Daly (no relation) who had a large dressmaking business in Limerick's main street, O'Connell Street.[19]

Clarke now considered returning to the United States, and wrote to John Devoy to see about engaging in a lecture tour there, as Daly had done very successfully in the winter of 1897-8. Meanwhile, still sore at the disappointment over Rathdown, he agreed to join the Daly family in Kilkee, County Clare, a traditional summer resort for Limerick's middle classes. Here his relationship with Kathleen deepened, although the only real privacy they could find was by taking very early morning walks along the cliffs. The other sisters were inquisitive, but largely unaware of what was impending; when Tom and Kathleen announced their engagement within a few days of his arrival, the news burst like a bombshell. Mrs Daly in particular seemed unwilling to let her daughter marry a prematurely aged man, with apparently few qualifications or talents and little immediate chance of earning a living, and twenty years older to boot. Even Uncle John, Clarke's closest friend, seems to have been antagonistic to the match, judging from references in Kathleen's letters to Clarke after he had returned to Dublin.

Indeed, Kathleen seems to have endured an enormous amount of criticism and teasing, and was driven to distraction by her family in the following months. Her solace lay in the almost daily correspondence with her fiancé. The letters were now addressed to 'Tom' ('It does seem very strange to be addressing you this way') and signed 'Kathleen'. He often addresses her by her pet name, Kattie (sometimes 'Katty'). As Foy and Barton put it, 'in Kathleen he had found a perfect soulmate whose ferocious political commitment matched his own, who worshipped him and gave him the support that sustained him for the rest of his life'.[20]

Clarke did his best to comfort her over the teasing of her family: 'I won't of course say a syllable to U.J. [Uncle John] about his humbugging – I'd like to but your wish is law in the matter (and I'm inclined to think in most things to me – if not in all things)'. And he was enduring a certain amount of family interest himself: 'Mrs Hart [was] telling futures with the cards … "Oh Tom loves a fair woman, she's dear to you and you are thinking a good deal about her – she is much in your thoughts …" I looked up, enquired if she was a widow. But faith I was afraid they'd see in my face that some fair woman was in my thoughts'.[21]

Now an engaged man, hoping to be married as soon as possible, Clarke placed all his hopes in John Devoy. John Daly, after all, had come home from the United States with enough money to set up his bakery, and provide a degree of security for his large number of dependants. However, Clarke soon had bad news from Devoy; his plans were rejected, and no help at all was offered. From Tom and Kathleen's letters, it is clear that this was a devastating blow to him. He bursts out that he had built everything on this lecture tour, all his hopes and dreams of marriage and a home. Kathleen comforts him as well as she can, and points out that if he had not been optimistic about his American plan he would never have dared to speak to her of love or marriage. He might have left her brokenhearted in Kilkee, embarrassed at having thrown herself at a man who seemingly did not want her. She made it clear that no matter where he went or what he did, she would go with him, and be proud to do so.

Gerard MacAtasney gives a cogent explanation of what might otherwise seem very odd behaviour on Devoy's part. Helping John Daly with a lecture tour had been a very different matter for Clan na Gael. Daly had a known pedigree; a participant in the 1867 Fenian rising, he had later been arrested for causing disturbances at a Home Rule meeting in 1876, and had become an IRB Head Centre for Connacht. He had been a famous prisoner, and an even more famous ex-prisoner, and was a great propaganda coup for the republican movement. He was extrovert and gregarious, and a gifted public speaker – indeed, he could go on for hours. This was more appreciated in that period than it would be now, and his speeches can sound bombastic and repetitive to a generation used to brisk sound-bites. He loved every moment of his tour; he was particularly impressed by his companion on the platforms, the beautiful young activist Maud Gonne.[22]

Tom Clarke, on the other hand, was just one of a number

of minor members of Clan na Gael who had been arrested for dynamiting activities. No-one really noticed his imprisonment until its later stages, after most of the others had been released. The Amnesty Association only campaigned seriously on his behalf when Daly took up Clarke's cause on his own release. His long endurance fuelled their propaganda. Besides, Clarke was a man of diffident and retiring personality; it was very unlikely that he could emulate Daly's impressive success, bringing thousands of excited Irish Americans to their feet.

John Daly did all he could on his friend's behalf, and was clearly very annoyed by Devoy's behaviour, writing to Clarke, 'All I can, or will say now Tom is never say die. We lived through a bloody sight worse than the cold indifference of Mr Devoy and his friends'.[23] Nothing worked, and Clarke faced a very bitter disappointment. He apparently seems to have considered going to South Africa, to fight for the Boers in their second war against the British (1899-1902), but in the end turned back to America, where he had lived before. Devoy could hardly refuse to give him some help once he was there, and if he got a job he could start planning his marriage. Both he and Kathleen felt strongly that they would do best side by side, supporting one another – if one could not work, the other would. Their whole lives together worked in this way, and she was always a great source of strength to him.

Clarke and his sister Maria sailed for the United States in

October 1899. Kathleen was very cast down at the thought of the distance that was to lie between them, but hopeful that she could join him before long. He obtained work as a pattern-maker in the Cameron Pump Works on 23rd East Street, New York – his prison training was standing to him at last. The foreman, Maurice Allen, was a Clan na Gael member. Clarke earned thirty-five dollars a week here, and was also employed by the Clan as a night clerk at fifteen dollars a week.[24]

He was lionised to a certain extent in New York: 'The Tyrone Ladies Association of New York made a great ado over me after I came here and presented me with a life-size bust (in oil) of me as I was before going to prison … there's precious little resemblance to the original in that picture. All the same Maria has it here in the room'.[25] In May, the Tyrone Men's Association put him on the arrangement committee for an excursion honouring him, with the added responsibility of writing it up for the newspapers.[26] Kathleen writes to him about her visit to his mother and sister; she was nervous about it at first, but decided she liked them immensely, although she found his mother very abrupt.[27]

In August 1900, Clarke was suddenly contacted by the Amnesty Association in Dublin, urging him to return home and apply for the position of superintendent of the Dublin Abattoirs, with a salary of £150 per annum and a house attached. He was very reluctant to give up his settled employment in New York for a promise which might not work out, but the telegrams from Dublin were extremely insistent, and in the end he resigned from the pump works and headed for Dublin, staying again in his mother's lodging house. The nationalist members of Dublin City Council were confident their plan would succeed, but the open vote was replaced by a closed ballot, and Clarke's candidacy was defeated.

In New York, his jobs had been held open for him, so he was able to resume his modest wages, and begin to plan for Kathleen to join him. Her family would not allow her to travel to America on her own, so she had to wait till a suitable travelling companion could be found. It was hoped she could travel with Maud Gonne, who was planning an American lecture tour. Uncle John was meant to be contacting Gonne on Kathleen's behalf, but, always a reluctant letter-writer, he apparently dragged his feet, much to Clarke's irritation: 'He ought to realize that although it may not be of any pressing importance to him it is of the greatest importance to you and I. Kattie I feel mad with him. He ought to remember the centre of the universe is not at all times himself'.[28] Old loyalties temporarily gave way to new, under the stress of a lover's impatience.

John Daly was invited to speak at St Patrick's Day celebrations in New York, 17 March 1901, and persuaded Kathleen to wait until then and travel with him. All hopes were now pinned on spring 1901 for their wedding, and their letters are filled with happy dreams and plans. Kathleen found her sisters and mother bemused by the urgency of her wish to travel so far from home, to marry a comparative stranger; as she said wryly, 'I'd do the same if the case was anyone else's'.[29] She could not convince them that Tom was no stranger to her, but the love of her life. She apparently told her mother that even if she had to play a hurdy-gurdy and wear a shawl over her shoulders (i.e. travel the roads) she was still going to marry him.[30]

All plans were thrown up in the air by an unlucky chance. The wife of James Egan, Clarke's erstwhile prison comrade, was badly injured while crossing a street in Dublin by two *Freeman's Journal* delivery vans; one knocked her down, the other rolled over her, according to Kathleen. No bones were broken, but she had a wound on her hip, and injuries to her spine.[31] The Egans sued the newspaper for damages, refusing to accept an offer of £1,050. Since Kathleen had been with Mrs Egan, she was an important eye-witness; she would be unable to travel until the case had been heard. Her sister Agnes 'encouraged' her by hoping that she would not 'get my thick tongue as I always do when I'm nervous and say everything wrong'.[32] Agnes and Kathleen were not always on good terms, although they had worked together.

Her letters to Tom indicate rising levels of frustration as the case went to trial in January 1901, and Clarke postponed the piano he was intending to hire for her.[33] The Egans won their judgement, but the *Freeman's Journal* threatened to appeal, which raised the spectre of a delay till September. Kathleen went back to Limerick for a time; 'Madge has got a bicycle ... and has me nearly killed running after her, teaching her ... I'd never learn, I'm too nervous of falling'. Her mother was annoying her with superstitions: 'Mama has some superstition about people marrying in May – the most unlucky month of the year ... I hate superstition – are you superstitious?'[34]

Uncle John had to travel to New York on his own, and tried to comfort his old friend, but there was only one person Clarke really wanted to see. Kathleen possessed her soul in patience a while longer ('Last Friday was my birthday and I was 23 years ... it frightens me to be getting old so fast'),[35] but the newspaper was finally refused a new trial in May, and she sailed for New York with Mr and Mrs Egan in July.

They were met at the landing-stage by Tom and Maria, and Kathleen travelled on a subway for the first time. In the excitement of this, she left behind on the seat a handbag containing all the money she had, 'quite a large sum', and of course it was never recovered.[36] The money was the profits of the dressmaking business she had run with her sister Agnes in Limerick. Indeed, Agnes was left high and dry by Kathleen's departure, and according to family sources never received her share of the business profits.

They all stayed at the Vanderbilt Hotel for a night, as the

wedding had been arranged for the following day, 16 July. Kathleen's luggage could not be found, so she got married in a frock belonging to Maria that was too small for her; it 'barely covered my knees, at a time when frocks were worn almost touching the ground. What did clothes matter, anyhow; off I went to the church …' They were married in St Augustine's Church by the Rev JA Talbot. The best man was a friend of Clarke's, Major John MacBride, just back from the Boer War, and the other witness was a Catherine McFadden. John Devoy also attended.[37]

Clarke had planned a week in Atlantic City, but Kathleen could not travel without her luggage (it was found some days later), so they spent their honeymoon in Tom's apartment in the Bronx, 1559 Brook Avenue. He had to go back to work the following week. Kathleen admits that she found the heat of New York prostrating, and the silence and loneliness of her little flat hard to bear after the large, noisy household she was used to. Moving around her apartment, Kathleen had to wear slippers to avoid disturbing the neighbours downstairs.

Life in Brooklyn and the Bronx for the large immigrant population was a matter of high, narrow overcrowded houses, shared toilet and washing facilities, and ceaseless noise and traffic in the streets. Newspaper reports of scalded children, frequent road accidents and accidental burnings from gas stoves reveal some of the prevailing conditions. Tom and Kathleen soon moved to 175 Russell Avenue, Greenpoint,

Brooklyn, to be nearer his place of work.[38]

Kathleen persuaded her husband to give up his night-time clerical work for Clan na Gael, but he maintained his involvement in the republican movement by becoming president of the Greenpoint Clan na Gael club, organising performances of Irish music and dancing. He started a journal called *The Clansman*, 'a real propaganda Irish-Ireland publication', with the slogan 'Total Separation. Ireland as Independent Republic'.[39] He was also involved in organising the celebrations of the anniversary of the birth of Robert Emmet, always an annual Clan na Gael highpoint; a note to Daniel Cohalan is scribbled at the back of a flyer for this event, to be held on 2 March 1902.[40]

Their first son was born on 13 June 1902, and Tom was delighted at the prospect of a son following him to fight for Ireland's freedom. The child was christened John Daly Clarke, and always known as 'Daly'. According to Kathleen's memoir, following Daly's birth, Clarke, now a full American citizen, sat for a civil service exam and passed it, but a friend advised him not to follow up on it – if questions were asked about his antecedents, he might be deported as an ex-felon. Kathleen was very angry at this; obviously Clarke's citizenship papers were in order, or he would not have been allowed to take the exam, so what was the problem? Tom took the advice, however, and Kathleen was left to regret the chance of an easier job, with steady hours and better money.[41] Kathleen's memoir may have got the date of this disappointment wrong; Tom Clarke's citizenship certificate is actually dated 2 November 1905.[42]

When Daly was eight months old, Clarke lost his job. Maurice Allen was dismissed from Cameron's, and all the men he had employed were dismissed with him. Kathleen, always a provident woman, had saved some money, and with this, and some help from her sister Madge, she bought an ice-cream and candy store in Greenpoint. She probably had some shopkeeping experience from Daly's Bakery, but she was a skilled and experienced dressmaker and a fully qualified tailor, and it seems odd that she did not turn in this direction. However, it would probably have taken her quite a long time to build up an adequate clientele, and perhaps American fashions were different from what she was used to. While she worked long hours in what must have been a low-profit enterprise (presumably with Daly in a room behind the shop), Clarke roamed the streets for work. Indeed, he actually considered applying for a job as a street-sweeper, and in the depths of despair told his wife he had been better off in Portland prison, where he had not had to beg for work.[43]

This time, John Devoy did help him. While he had been working at the Clan HQ, largely as Devoy's private secretary, they had built up a close relationship, and respected one another's abilities. Several of Tom's letters on Devoy's behalf, about arrangements and attendance at meetings, can be found in the archives of the American-Irish Historical Society in New York. Devoy had planned for some time to set up a weekly newspaper for the Irish republican constituency in America, and now approached Tom to act as general manager. This was the *Gaelic American*, which was to become an extremely influential channel for Irish revolutionary ideas. Devoy himself was editor, and the paper was launched in September 1903.

Clarke canvassed advertisers, resourced news from Irish papers, wrote sub-leaders and chased other Clan members for articles. He was a stickler for proper grammar and spelling: when John Carroll, an aspiring contributor, brought him an article, 'he handed it right back to me, saying rather sternly, "John Mitchel would turn in his grave if he knew you spelled his name with two 'l's"'.[44] As Le Roux puts it, he was 'not only a slave to duty, but the hard-worked servant of a hard-working and hard-worked master'. Le Roux adds (obviously from his talks with Kathleen) that Clarke 'made use of every man's ability, and never turned down a practical scheme or a piece of useful work'.[45] These 'personnel management' skills later proved essential in the lead-up to the Easter Rising.

For the next three years, Tom and Kathleen's lives followed a fairly tranquil course. They sold the ice-cream and candy store and moved to 99th Street in Brooklyn. As nationalist activists, they mounted protest meetings and pickets against anti-Irish plays or shows. When all the Irish societies were brought together as the 'United Irish American Societies', Clarke became corresponding secretary, organising the Brooklyn section. The aim of this group was to oppose a proposed Anglo-American alliance, and Irish nationalist pressure was one of the reasons it was ultimately defeated. A later attempt at an Anglo-American Peace Treaty was also defeated, in 1905, with the help of German-American socie-ties.[46]

Another of Clarke's enthusiasms was to track down the forgotten graves of Irish Fenians. Over forty such graves were found, and the IRB Veterans' Association began to hold annual commemorations for them, raising their own profile in the process. Clarke then established an annual pilgrimage to the grave of Matilda Tone, wife of the noted United Irish-man leader Theobald Wolfe Tone, which was in Greenwood Cemetery. He also joined the military wing of Clan na Gael, called the Irish Volunteers, and was appointed to the rank of regimental adjutant in the Second Infantry on 1 January 1906.[47] They often went into the country for rifle practice days, and Kathleen and young Daly would accompany them for the fresh air.[48]

However, Kathleen's health was never good after Daly's birth. During one serious bout of illness, Clarke's sister Maria (who had married Edward Fleming on 15 September 1901) had to move in with them to help with the nursing. In summer 1904, letters indicate that Kathleen and Daly spent about three months at St Michael's Villa, Englewood, New Jersey, run by a religious order; this seems to have provided fresh-air holidays and convalescent care, but the reason for her stay there is never made clear. She writes cheerfully of her newly-found piety: 'I say my Angelus twice a day, go to church twice a day for prayer. Daly will stay in church if they have music but not otherwise…'[49] However, she found it irksome to be away from home too long, and became bored with the quiet and the religious atmosphere: '…if I had another week to stay here I'd be found drowned'. Hoping to improve her health, the Clarkes moved further out, to the end of the Fulton Street L-line in Brooklyn. Tom then established the Brooklyn Gaelic Society, and Kathleen and Daly would attend the regular lectures, debates and social evenings.

In 1905, further concern was caused by the serious illness of Daly, aged three; he caught diphtheria, then a life-threatening infection which, if survived, often had repercussions in later life. After a six-week period of quarantine, Kathleen and Daly travelled to Limerick for three months of rest. Summer was spent in Kilkee, and by October Kathleen was feeling a good deal better. Daly was being spoilt by all the attention given him, especially by Uncle John; she worried he was getting too cheeky, but otherwise felt it had been a useful break. However, she and Tom missed one another terribly, and she was obviously keen to get back to Brooklyn. The *Clansman* produced a souvenir programme of the Clan na Gael annual Picnic and Athletic Games, held at Ridgewood Park on the 4th of July, 1906; such events must have provided happy diversions.[50]

Kathleen soon became ill again, and this time her doctor advised a move right out of the city. With the help of John Daly and his niece Madge (who in fact managed all his business), the Clarkes bought a small market garden farm called Manor Culverton, in Manorville, Long Island. Tom had to resign from the *Gaelic American*, and the pair began to grow crops such as cauliflowers for market, with more hope than experience. Kathleen bathes this period of their lives in a rosy light, and it is clear that she was really happy with her rural existence, despite non-laying chickens, forest fires and large snakes – one of which threatened Daly until his father chopped it to bits with a shovel.[51] Tom himself seems to have enjoyed the rural lifestyle, and was very pleased with himself for inventing a spray to kill flea-beetles in his potato crop.[52]

Storm clouds were gathering in Europe, and by 1907 it was clear that Clarke was listening to the news with a growing hope that England was going to be drawn into war, providing an opportunity for Ireland to strike a blow for her freedom. It always galled him that Ireland had not tried to rise during the Boer War, surely missing a golden opportunity. Kathleen's memoir describes his growing tension, and urge to return home, along with her own reluctance to see this happen, and her fears for the future. She said to him, 'You have done as much as any country could expect of a man, and small thanks or appreciation you received'. He would not listen, protesting that he never worked for thanks, but because the cause was right.[53]

She also worried about the fact that her husband was a free citizen in America, but would be a ticket-of-leave man once he was back on 'British' territory. He would risk being returned to prison at any time, which would surely kill him. She was fighting to protect the life they had, and her little family, and sensed that nothing would be the same once they saw Ireland again.

However, as MacAtasney points out, Tom's need to fight for Ireland was probably not the whole story behind their return. The market gardening was not successful; Tom would have needed to be a younger, stronger man to succeed, and later letters indicate that they left Long Island with a load of debt to be repaid. Madge Daly had helped them financially during their American years, and the deeds of Manor Culverton were registered in John Daly's name. Now Madge offered to set them up in business if they would come home.[54] John Devoy was obviously sorry to lose his right-hand man, but promised Tom all possible help to forward the republican cause in Ireland, and gave him letters to introduce him to the IRB.

Tom, Kathleen and Daly Clarke arrived at the port of Cobh, County Cork, on 10 December 1907, where they were met by Madge and Uncle John.[55] The family was, of course, thrilled to see them back, and efforts were made to encourage them to stay in Limerick, but Tom wanted to be at the centre of events in Dublin, where the IRB had its HQ. It is probable also that Kathleen preferred to be out of reach of her rather claustrophobic family circle. Tom's sister Hannah ran a small newsagency and tobacconist shop, and had encouraged him to go into the same business.

It was decided that Kathleen and young Daly would remain in Limerick until Tom could get established in Dublin. The next few months were long for them, as their daily letters indicate. Kathleen was pregnant again, feeling out of sorts, fending off the curiosity of her sisters and mother: 'I mean to dodge Mama, also Eileen, she is just dead with curiosity…'. She was worrying again about Daly being spoilt – 'he is so saucy, he is getting worse every day, when one won't give way to him another will, when one is out with him the rest are in…' The child obviously longed to return to Long Island; he was wildly excited when some photographs of their farm arrived, and was very angry when he heard someone say they would never go back. Kathleen admitted she had not yet had the nerve to tell him so herself, and hoped he would gradually forget it. He was getting cheekier: 'He told Uncle John and Madge a few days ago if they were not nice to him he'd go to Dublin to his Granny Clarke'.[56]

She missed her husband desperately: 'Like you, I cannot talk to anyone in the same unreserved way I can to you…' Earlier in January she had written, 'I'm afraid Maple Farm spoiled me, having you all the time to myself; I want it to be the same all the time, I'm cross and crotchety that it's not so. I feel as if two or three months is an eternity…' It is clear that their relationship was very close and affectionate: 'I wouldn't if I were you be calling myself names for writing nice things to your wife — things you'd say to her in bed every night if you got a chance…they make the world seem a much brighter place to her that she has a smile that won't come off all this day and couldn't be cross with anyone, for anything, now'. This was in response to a letter from Tom which said, 'Life without you Katty wouldn't be worth living…There now, I am perhaps writing like a sentimental ass. Anyway if I didn't feel as I do about my wee wife I would be an ass — so there'.[57]

Meanwhile Tom was back living with his mother and Hannah at 176 Great Britain Street, and was pleased with his reception there: 'Both H and the old lady can't do half enough to try and make me feel at home. Did I tell you the old lady said the first time we met that I was not a day older looking…She stands it well — not a bit changed in appearance but I believe she is not nearly as blunt and harsh in manner [as before]'.'I'm still her white-haired boy and it is laughable to hear her ruling against Hannah whenever she gets a chance in my favour. My mother seems to me to be a great deal clearer and not so queer as when I left for America'. But as Kathleen herself was also finding, family was not enough for him: 'I am happy when I am with you. I can't help it but with Hannah I am with a stranger who doesn't really know me and I can't feel happy or content.'[58]

Clarke started searching for a suitable shop in a central location, and found what he wanted before Christmas, at 55 Amiens Street, near a railway station – a good location, with a lot of passing trade. The rent was £36 a year, and there was one room behind, into which he now moved. Kathleen was uneasy about this: 'It will be like while I was home last, tea and bread and bread and tea…you're not made of iron and with the shop to look after alone you cannot afford to be sick or even out of sorts; so don't be in a rush to leave your mother'.[59] Tom spent Christmas in Limerick, then returned to supervise the renovation of the shop; all the costs were being subsidised by Madge Daly.

He had a large gold '55' attached to the middle of the front window, which attracted a lot of attention – he had probably seen similar window decorations in New York. Hannah disapproved of it: 'Nobody did it in Dublin and everybody was talking about it'.[60] He assured her that this was the point. He also hoped to start a nationalist newspaper, but was unable to raise the funding at this time. He was already worried about the amount they owed the Daly family: 'Sometimes when I get athinking of the load already on us and of the generous way John is and has been standing by us, I feel my heart getting very heavy and that there is no one in the world outside yourself that I could hope to expect such proof of generous friendship.'[61]

Daly's health caused some alarm in February, just after his father had made a flying visit to Limerick. The doctor 'said he was bloodless and it would take at least three months to bring him round, he is tired and crotchety all the time, and is eating nothing, today he seems feverish all day'. Two days later Kathleen wrote that the doctor 'was at a loss to account for the sudden rises in temperature he gets…the fever seems to be all gone from him today'. She later surmised that Daly might have had a touch of malaria, which he had suffered from several times on Maple Farm; an Irish doctor would know little about it, and she had treated it herself with quinine and lemons. She was impatient for her next child to be born: 'I have everything ready for my own affair, not another stitch to put, so the sooner it comes off the better I like it'.

Their second son, called Thomas for his father, was born in Limerick on 3 March 1908. Tom was thrilled, but couldn't leave the shop, which had opened in early February, to see him. Instead he wrote, in response to John's telegram, 'When I read the telegram I dropped what I was doing and went back into the room and burst out crying. I still feel choking ... Kiss the little stranger over and over again for me'.[62] Kathleen had suggested Clarke's brother Alfred as godfather, but Tom was reluctant: 'I wrote Alf some time ago but like Uncle J he doesn't love sitting down to write letters and of course I haven't got any reply'.[63]

Clarke had been warned that he might be opening at a bad time, as many people gave up tobacco for Lent, but he was pleasantly surprised at the regular stream of customers. He was of course in an excellent position, on a busy city street. Hannah was being a great support, introducing Tom to the various travellers in newspapers and tobacco products; this surprised Kathleen, who had felt Hannah was antago-nistic towards her, but she was very pleased that the family was working together. She wrote, 'Uncle John says he thinks with Hannah that there is no small business pays as well as the tobacco and cigars. I am quite surprised and really pleased that Hannah is so friendly'.[64]

Clarke wrote excited accounts of his daily routine, and seemed very content in his new profession: 'several times this evg. I have had ½ doz people at one time in the shop – it looks well'.[65] Well-advised by Hannah, he kept a wide stock: 'All told I have 38 different brands of cigarettes alone. I have not turned away any customer by not having what he asked for'. He was feeling overworked: 'Have you any idea of how busy I am kept? Checking off papers from ½ dozen sources, keeping track of unsold copies and talking to customers etc

etc. I miss you very much in all this'.[66]

Kathleen took some time to recover from the birth, and had to stay in bed. Restless and crotchety, she refused to allow the baby to be taken out for a walk by the servant Hannah – she couldn't bear to let him out of her sight. She was irritated by her family's fussing: 'One would think the way they talk that I was a helpless individual…but the interesting invalid is not a role to my liking'.[67] She had already been annoyed by her mother's insistence that she be 'churched' (a purification blessing after childbirth) before going out anywhere, and that she would not have good health until this had been done. Her own relationship with religion was detached, to say the least, as was Clarke's.

Money was occasionally a problem: 'I had to pay the dentist 10 shillings and I must get Daly new shoes, he wants them badly, so if you can send me £1 some day next week, there is no particular hurry about it…' Her sister Madge helped out from time to time, but Kathleen was torn between gratitude to her, and not wishing to be under an obligation. At all events, the baby was thriving: 'he is as strong a baby as you'd see for his age, he lifts his head straight up after the bath', and was 'a good-tempered little darling'. In fact, she was so besotted that she insisted she'd have no more babies: 'they get too great a grip on one…once I get them it's misery to have them out of my sight'.[68]

Kathleen finally left Limerick in June or July, having agreed to leave the baby for a few weeks – the family had wanted her to do so for several months, and it annoyed her intensely that they could think it would cost her nothing to do so. She had badly wanted to leave earlier, but was afraid of being a burden on her husband if she wasn't well enough to cope. There were now two children to look after, as well as the shop, and they also needed to search for a proper home; she would need all her strength. She worried about Tom's health, and felt he wasn't looking after himself; he had a recurrent stomach problem, and his feet were feeling the pressure of standing in the shop all day.

It had been suggested earlier in the year that one of Kathleen's younger sisters, Annie, could come to Dublin as a boarder with Tom and Kathleen, and get a job there – they would look after her better than a boarding house would.[69] This scheme had not been followed through; Madge had felt that Annie was not strong enough to leave home. The job Annie had in Limerick (unspecified in the letters) gave her very little pay, and apparently the air was always foul. While the Clarkes were still searching for a home in Dublin, they heard that Annie had died suddenly of typhoid fever, aged 21. Typhus is a disease which lives in conditions of dirt and squalor, facilitated by crowded conditions; it is carried by fleas and ticks.[69]

The Clarkes hastened down to Limerick again, to the devastated family. Back in Dublin after the funeral, Tom himself came down with typhoid fever, and was seriously ill for some weeks in the Mater Hospital. Kathleen had to run the business by herself, knowing little about it, and her brother Ned came up from Limerick to help her. In her memoir, she says, 'Ned was a delightful companion, cheerful and full of quiet fun. He would not let me be downhearted, took care of Daly and in many other ways helped me … All the time I was afraid Tom would die like my sister'.[71]

When Tom had recovered, he went down to Limerick to convalesce, and also spent a month in Crookhaven, County Cork, with several members of the Daly family and his baby son Tom. Writing in September, he says, 'between beef tea or chicken broth and egg flip and meals I seem to keep eating almost all the time…I must have added another 6lbs.' By the end of September he was looking forward to being home: 'Every one of the family seemed anxious to do everything in their power to build me up and make me strong and give me a pleasant time…Experiences like this would prevent one from losing faith in the unselfish kindness of men and women'.

Chapter Four

• • • • • • •

Shopkeeper and Republican
1908-1914

The Clarke family had arrived back to an Ireland which
was more open to nationalist ideas than ever before. A
cultural revolution was informing the population about the
relics of ancient Ireland which still survived – archaeological
remains were being studied, use of the Irish language was
being encouraged, Irish music and dancing and games were
being brought to the fore.

The passing of the Catholic Emancipation act in 1829 had
ushered in a resurgence of faith and devotion. Large Catholic
churches were now built on main streets, leaving behind the
little back-street chapels to which Catholics had been confined. A sense of Irishness, defined as Catholicism, was developing; Protestantism was equated with being English, and a
gap began to widen. This growing nationalism was badly set
back by the disaster of the Great Famine (1845-49) which
saw the destruction of hundreds of small communities, the

deaths of over a million people and the emigration of at least a million more – a pattern of dispersal that encouraged more than two million others to emigrate over the next fifty years.

The Irish language, already damaged by an English system of education, was almost wiped out in some parts of the country. The call for separation was fuelled by the apparent contempt for Irish lives; would English peasants have been allowed to starve the same way? Separatism, both political and militant, developed rapidly, but the country was not ready for the militant response; the Young Ireland rebellion of 1848 failed completely. Nor was the 1867 Fenian uprising a success, but it lit a spark in America which became extremely influential. The anger of Irish republican emigrants such as O'Donovan Rossa and Clan na Gael, and their commitment to getting rid of English rule at any cost, was driven by memories of the Famine, and the destruction it had caused. John Daly and Tom Clarke may have been born too late to witness the Famine, but their parents and grandparents had lived through it, Daly's in County Limerick and Clarke's in Leitrim and Tipperary.

As the country slowly began to recover economically, a cultural revival late in the century was spearheaded by the establishment of the Gaelic Athletic Association (GAA) in 1884, which set itself to revive old Irish games such as football and hurling, and to introduce them to schools instead of the English sports of cricket and rugby. The Irish

Republican Brotherhood, the militant organisation linked to Clan na Gael, had an early presence in the GAA. Then came the Gaelic League in 1893, an organisation dedicated to the 'de-anglicization' of Ireland and the revival of the Irish language. It held classes, lectures and debates, and attracted large numbers of enthusiastic young people to its ranks. Although a largely urban body, it reached people all over the country through its newspaper, *An Claidheamh Soluis* ('Sword of Light'), and the publication of Irish poems, stories and plays. It was strictly non-political. The following decade saw the foundation of the Irish National Literary Society (1892) and the Irish Literary Theatre (1898), later the Abbey Theatre, both aiming to promote Irish writing and drama.

This cultural activity was led by an elite group of artists, poets and writers, but the aim was to revive a sense of Irishness in the country as a whole, and the GAA was hugely successful at a popular level. The cultural revolution was not necessarily separatist – many of its protagonists were unionist in sympathy – but the message was of an Ireland which had been coerced into accepting English cultural norms. A superior Irish cultural heritage had been in danger of being lost, and was now being proudly reclaimed.

This ferment of nationalism obviously provided fertile ground for a republican movement, and that movement was pushed further into militancy over the next few years by political developments such as the Home Rule campaign, the growth of a militant unionist movement in Ulster, the Dublin Lockout of 1913 (from which grew the Irish Citizen Army) and the outbreak of the Great War in 1914. Tom Clarke, despite his age, his long absence from Ireland and his small-scale, domesticated image, became central to the development of republican activity during these years.

Clarke arrived in Dublin with letters of recommendation from John Devoy, and was immediately admitted into IRB circles. He also had many valuable contacts in the North of Ireland. These included Bulmer Hobson, born in 1883, with whom he had corresponded from New York, Dr Pat McCartan (born 1878), Diarmuid Lynch (born 1878) and Denis McCullough (born 1883). Hobson and McCullough had in 1905 founded the Dungannon Clubs, republican, separatist and non-sectarian societies, and folded these clubs into the Sinn Féin League in 1907. Sinn Féin, an organisation developed under Hobson and Arthur Griffith between 1905 and 1908, proposed a model of Irish independence based on a dual monarchy, with a separate parliament for Ireland, and a protectionist economic policy. The Easter Rising was later described by the British as a 'Sinn Féin' rebellion, but Sinn Féin had nothing to do with violent separatism.

Another northern activist was Seán MacDiarmada, born in Leitrim in 1884, who was an organiser for Sinn Féin when he met Tom Clarke in 1908. Clarke himself had joined Sinn Féin, as IRB policy was to infiltrate as many nationalist organisations as possible, but he persuaded MacDiarmada to move to the IRB instead. MacDiarmada became an extremely effective IRB organiser, and also a close friend to Clarke and Kathleen, both of whom admired him greatly. He was a very attractive character, always in good humour, and an intense worker. MacDiarmada, Hobson, McCartan and others moved from the north to Dublin from about 1908, sensing that the time was ripe for consolidation. Denis McCullough lost his two closest friends, Hobson and Mac-Diarmada, and had to carry on on his own, 'as there were no others of my vintage left with whom I could co-operate'.[1]

Tom Clarke, already older than the young people by whom he was now surrounded, appeared even more aged because of his weakened sight and hearing, and his stooped figure, but his long years of imprisonment made him an icon. The younger generation appreciated what he had suffered, and were impressed by his reluctance to retire from the fray, and his commitment to a new future for Ireland, at whatever cost. He established his position quietly, gradually accustoming nationalist groups to his presence, and sounding out young men and women whom he felt would be energetic and reliable.

Meanwhile he ran his little shop in Amiens Street, and in 1909 expanded into a second shop, 75A Parnell Street, at the foot of Dublin's main street, Sackville (later O'Connell) Street. This address was destined to become a central meet-

ing-point for republican activists, and a hotbed of revolutionary activity which was constantly under surveillance by the
Dublin Metropolitan Police. Friends coming to visit at night,
before closing time, would find Tom Clarke sitting on a chair,
erect, his hands on his knees, as he must have sat as a convict.
'Nothing resembled a prison cell more than this small shop…
it was so narrow that there was hardly more room to sit on
the public side of the narrow counter than on the other side'.[2]
His instinct was always to be retiring and unobtrusive; even in
photographs, he rarely looks straight at the camera.

Clarke took his business very seriously, always maintain-
ing a good stock of newspapers and tobacco products, and
alert to any opportunity to increase sales. When a scandal
broke over the theft of the Irish Crown Jewels from Dublin
Castle, in August 1908, he laid in extra stocks of the one
newspaper which covered it. This attracted the attention
of the DMP's detectives, because publication of the affair
had been censored, but they did not close him down. When
election results came out, he would order in several dozen
extra newspapers; if a customer asked for a particular tobacco
unknown to him, he would take care to supply it. This was
his living, and that of his family, so of course he had to work
hard at it, but it pleased him to run it efficiently. To begin
with he worked from 9 am till 11 pm, seven days a week, but
gradually was able to employ assistants.

He was particularly kind towards the little newspaper

boys, who came to him for papers to sell. He admired them for their courage and good humour, despite their problems, 'out late and early – poorly clad, poorly fed – in wet and cold', recalls PS O'Hegarty. 'And they returned his kindness and love in full measure. I often saw a little lad rush into his shop with a bundle of papers under his arm, pull a sour apple or a dirty sweet out of his pocket and offer it to Tom with a "Here you are Mr Clarke, I kept it for you". Tom always took the proffered gift with courtesy and thanks…When they had no money for papers they came to Tom for credit. They always got it, and rarely was his trust in them misplaced'.[3] Clarke was certainly kept busy with the two shops, and with disentangling the Long Island property and its debts – it was taking a long time to sell. And his family continued to grow; his third son, Emmet, was born on 13 August 1909, in the Rotunda Hospital.

Clarke maintained an active presence in Sinn Féin, although he refused to stand as a Sinn Féin candidate in local elections; still 'on licence', he had to keep a low profile. As president of the North Dock Ward branch of Sinn Féin, he proposed a successful motion in April 1909 deploring the prospect of Irish trade unions seeking closer link with British unions, and asserting a need for 'a federation of trades bodies in Ireland that will be absolutely independent of English control'.[4] He was also president of a pipers' club associated with a Gaelic Football club in the North Wall area of

Dublin.[5] However, his main involvement was still with the IRB. From the time he left New York, Clan na Gael had increased the amount of money they sent to the IRB, never less than $1,000 dollars at a time, according to John Devoy, and in all amounting to $100,000 before the Easter Rising, an enormous sum.[6]

In August 1909, Bulmer Hobson and Countess Constance Markievicz, a fiery activist from an Ascendancy background, founded Na Fianna Éireann, an Irish equivalent to the British Boy Scout movement.[7] It was under IRB control, and its manifesto made it clear that its object was to train boys up so that they could one day fight for Ireland. It took Clarke some time to trust Countess Markievicz; he was amused by her, but did not take her seriously until she became involved with the Fianna. He then helped her to get it started.[8]

In 1910, Tom and Kathleen closed 55A Amiens Street and rented a different shop in Amiens Street, No. 77, with living space overhead; they moved their home here from Drumcondra, where Daly had attended St Patrick's Christian Brothers School.

Having created a role for himself, Clarke's first definite move was to establish a republican newspaper. It would have to be very carefully written, because anything too obviously subversive would be closed down by the authorities. Funding was provided by John Daly and Dr Pat McCartan, and one shilling per month was levied on individual IRB members.[9] Some members of Clan na Gael visited John Daly in Limerick in October, 1910, and it seems likely they wished to oversee the launch of the new paper; perhaps they had provided some funding as well.[10]

The paper was to advocate a separatist policy, adhering to the non-sectarian principles of the United Irishmen. Clarke himself was too busy to act as editor, but according to his wife he had a veto at the meetings at which possible contributions were discussed. MacDiarmada was general manager; McCartan became editor. The first edition of *Irish Freedom* was published on 15 November, 1910; it began as a monthly, but later moved to weekly publication.[11] Politically, the Irish Parliamentary Party (IPP) had enormous popular support, and it was this 'constitutional nationalism' that the IRB were hoping to convert into something more militant.

Clarke also involved himself in commemorations of dead nationalist heroes, as he had done in New York. He took part in the annual pilgrimages to Wolfe Tone's grave in Bodenstown, and helped to establish support committees for the parents of one of the 'Manchester Martyrs', Fenians who had been executed in 1867. The IRB in general, however, was wary of public demonstrations; its aim was always to stay under the radar. Thomas Barry gives an example of its modus operandi: '[Cork Young Ireland Society]...was being held together by the remnants of the older IRB group in the city...On the instructions of Tom Clarke, Seán O'Sullivan,

Paddy Corkery and I went into the Young Ireland Society
and I was elected President. This was the normal method
by which the IRB influenced the policy and controlled the
activities of all National organisations. Our principal job in
the YIS was to ensure that the speaker at the annual Manchester Martyrs demonstration was an IRB man'.[12]

In November 1910, after a general election, the Irish Parliamentary Party (IPP), under John Redmond MP, found
itself holding the balance of power in the British Parliament.
The prospect of a Home Rule bill actually passing became a
possibility. This was a matter of concern to the IRB; the bulk
of the population would probably welcome Home Rule, but
it would never be the complete separation the IRB sought.
Home Rule would provide a parliament in Dublin, but many
important governmental functions would still be controlled
from London. However, Redmond and the IPP had worked
hard to achieve even this much, through several failed bills,
and they would not turn away from it now.

In July, 1911, King George V was to make an official royal
visit to Ireland. The IRB Supreme Council, mindful of the
need not to draw undue attention to itself, forbade its membership to make any public demonstration of protest at this
visit. The Council at this time was dominated by old-school
IRB men such as Fred Allan and John O'Hanlon, whose
activity was mainly confined to Dublin Corporation politics.
Allan, for example, would have to pay his respects to the

King because of his position as secretary to Dublin's Lord Mayor.

However, following a speech by Patrick Pearse at a Robert Emmet commemoration concert, Tom Clarke and Pat McCartan publicly opposed loyal addresses being made to the King, and were greeted with cheers. For this offence, the Supreme Council immediately sacked McCartan as editor of *Irish Freedom*, and threatened legal proceedings against the printers if they went ahead with the next issue. The printers told McCartan they would print the issue for him, but only if £100 was lodged with their solicitors for their own security. McCartan had only £20 available, and Clarke, as Treasurer of the Supreme Council, said he could not sign a cheque for £80 without using part of the IRB account. McCartan remembered, 'I begged him to give me the money…when I said I would go ahead alone [getting the money elsewhere], Tom said "That hurts, Pat" and lifted the keys of his shop from a nail and came out and got the £80'. The money was subsequently repaid by Joseph McGarrity, a Clan na Gael activist.[13]

McCartan and Clarke were apparently called to an IRB court-martial, the result of which was a general agreement that it had all been a misunderstanding.[14] Shortly afterwards, however, Fred Allan and Jack O'Hanlon resigned from the Supreme Council, and Allan's place as Secretary was filled by MacDiarmada. The IRB leadership was now almost completely in the hands of the younger men, backed by Clarke as Treasurer.[15] The IRB continued to operate under the cover of meetings of so-called 'Wolfe Tone Clubs', and PS O'Hegarty became editor of *Irish Freedom*.

During the king's visit, a huge reception was held for him in Phoenix Park. A nationalist counter-demonstration was organised at Wolfe Tone's grave in Bodenstown, which Clarke attended, leaving his wife to look after the shop. As groups of British soldiers and sailors returned from Phoenix Park through Sackville Street, they were confronted by a huge *Irish Freedom* poster outside the Clarke shop which read: 'Your concessions be damned! England!!! We want our country'. A large and angry crowd collected, and the poster was taken down and thrown into the shop. Kathleen brought it back out and re-hung it, announcing that she would call the police if anyone touched it again. It was a nervous time for her until Clarke came home, but the crowd gradually dispersed.[16] That Bodenstown demonstration marked the first time on which Patrick Pearse addressed a large crowd, invited by Clarke on MacDiarmada's recommendation. Pearse, a serious-minded young schoolteacher, seemed an unlikely revolutionary to Clarke, but he soon learned the young man's worth in terms of swaying public opinion, through both speeches and writing.

In 1911, Seán MacDiarmada, exhausted by months of travelling around the country, contracted polio, and was left with permanent damage to his hip. To aid his recuperation, he was welcomed at that haven for all republicans, John Daly's household in Limerick, and subsequently came to regard it as his second home. Despite the difference in age, he and Daly became close, and developed the greatest of respect for one another. It has been suggested that MacDiarmada had cynically decided to use Daly as a way into the inner circles of the IRB, but his letters to Daly and other family members express an unfeigned affection. MacDiarmada's own charm and ferocious activity were enough in themselves to win him trust and respect.

By 1911, Tom and Kathleen's businesses were successful enough to enable them to rent a house in St Patrick's Road, Drumcondra, a distinct step up from 'living above the shop'. This enabled them both to follow their interest in gardening which, according to Le Roux, was 'both a business and an art' for Clarke; he was always cheerful when working in his garden.[17] By now, Tom junior was attending Fairview National School, later followed by Emmet. Clarke's sister Hannah was still living with her mother at 176 Great Britain Street. His brother Alfred had come back from England with a wife and three children, and was living near Merchant's Quay; he worked as a time-keeper on the Paving Committee of Dublin Corporation.[18]

Family matters, financial and otherwise, kept Clarke busy. Writing to Devoy while sending him an outstanding $100 for his *Gaelic American* account, he confesses, '…sickness of one kind and another at home with us and its consequences in the shape of doctors' and surgeons' bills – together with the fact that my sister's business went wrong and I couldn't help giving her a hand, has … kept me at low water. As a matter of fact I am doing exceptionally well in business …and prospects look very promising … We have secured the Mansion House for 22 June (Coronation Day) to hold a nationalist demonstration – by way of celebrating Wolfe Tone's birthday…'[19]

His continual overworking often placed his health under strain. Between 24 April and 2 May 1912 he was writing to Kathleen from Limerick, where he was staying with Tom junior: 'I am feeling immensely improved – Every morning I have been up about 7 and go out – and do a walk along the Shannon bank – myself and Shawn the dog'.[20] Kathleen also needed the occasional rest, and spent part of the summer of 1912 in Limerick with her children. Clarke wrote to her about a change of staff in the shop – May was leaving for another job, and Lucy had been engaged 'on the basis of the talk you had with her. … I'll coach her until she gets her hand in … I hope next letter will tell me you have improved and that the children are well'.[21] On 22 July, he was able to report that Lucy 'is going on all right … I am getting the front of 75 Parnell Street washed and varnished tomorrow. It is looking very dingy at present'.

Behind these chatty letters, political movement was taking place. In Ulster, the unionist population was becoming increasingly agitated by the prospect of Home Rule, and of being ruled by a Dublin parliament. They were adamant that they wished to maintain the union with Britain, and feared being crushed under Popish laws. They threatened to withhold the payment of taxes to Britain, and 218,206 men signed a Solemn League and Covenant on 28 September 1912, some in blood. More than 200,000 women signed a similar pledge. The anti-Home Rule movement was led by Sir Edward Carson, a Dublin-born lawyer and Unionist MP for Dublin University, who was implacably opposed to Home Rule, and sought instead a separate government for Ulster.

As well as constitutional opposition, Carson advocated a threat of military force, to place more pressure on the British government. Founded in January 1913, the Ulster Volunteer Force (UVF) pledged itself to resist Home Rule by any means necessary. Prominent businessmen and dignitaries provided the finance, and funds flowed in from England and Scotland as well. In September 1913, the Ulster Unionist Council appointed what they called a Provisional Government for Ulster, and the UVF was designated as its official army.

The UVF ostensibly drilled legally, as most local magistrates were sympathetic and gave them permission to do so, but Carson proclaimed: 'Drilling is illegal, the Volunteers are illegal and the government knows they are illegal, and the government does not interfere with them'. Certainly the unionists seem to have been given a free hand; the British government was reluctant to inflame passions further, and turned a blind eye to what was obvious subversion. Carson knew very well that Home Rule would not be forced on Ulster; the Liberal government were pragmatists, and knew that the Home Rule bill could not be enacted until the issue of Ulster was addressed.[22]

All of this was eagerly observed from Dublin by Tom Clarke, who sensed a change in the political climate. Irish constitutional nationalists could see that their cherished Home Rule bill was under threat, and that the government might buckle under unionist pressure. Perhaps these people could now be persuaded to follow the unionist example, and start to fight for increased control of their own destiny. The IRB had been marking time for a couple of years, waiting for an opportunity to galvanise the population, and here it now was. Since the Ulster unionists had established their own private army, it was obvious that nationalist Ireland would have to do the same. Clarke wrote to John Devoy: 'At last we see tangible results from the patient, plodding work of sowing the seed. The tide is running strongly in our direction. *We have the rising generation.*'[23]

A huge public meeting was called for the night of 25 November 1913, at the Rotunda Rink in Dublin. Patrick

Pearse provided the justification: 'Ireland armed will make a better bargain with the Empire than Ireland unarmed'.[24] Also on the platform was Bulmer Hobson, but the IRB were not to be publicly identified with this new movement. Hobson became Secretary of the Irish Volunteers, the organisation which was founded that night. Clarke disapproved of Hobson taking such a prominent role, but was persuaded that an IRB presence among the committee officers was necessary to keep things moving in the right direction. Twelve other members of the committee were also IRB members, and Patrick Pearse, Joseph Plunkett and Thomas MacDonagh of the committee later joined the IRB. Plunkett, a poet, was editor of *The Irish Review*; MacDonagh, a Gaelic League member, was a teacher at Pearse's school, St Enda's. Chief-of-Staff of the Volunteers was Eoin MacNeill, a UCD professor and founder member of the Gaelic League, who had written the article which first suggested a nationalist military force. He supported the politics of Redmond and the IPP, but was convinced that the Home Rule movement needed to counter the militant noises coming from the North with its own force.

It seemed as though the IRB leaders were not really convinced about the reality of unionist opposition to Home Rule, and had no conception of the opposition they would have faced there if the rising had been successful. They welcomed the opportunity provided by the UVF, but scarcely appreciated the force of resentment behind it. Clarke, however, with his northern upbringing and his numerous northern contacts, must have known how appalled unionists would have been at the prospect of becoming part of an independent Irish non-Protestant state. And he was certainly kept informed in 1912 and 1913 by the young Bertie Smyllie, later editor of the *Irish Times*.

Smyllie, born in Glasgow and reared in Sligo, was a student at Trinity College, and frequently visited Clarke's shop. Smyllie's father, who ran a newspaper in the west of Ireland, came to an agreement with Clarke to allow the lad to draw on him for funds when necessary. 'Even when there was little or nothing to my parental credit he often advanced me a sovereign … and saved me from the Liffey, or at least from the pawnshops'. Smyllie was intrigued by the numerous young men who would visit, always going into the back room. He continues: 'I was a violent Carsonite in those far-off days, and often used to argue the Unionist toss with Tom Clarke when the two of us were alone in the shop'.[25] However, complete separatism was Clarke's creed, and the problem of unionism was ignored.

Unionism was not taken very seriously elsewhere either, judging from a letter from a County Cork solicitor, PJ Collins, to Daniel Cohalan in New York, dated 13 February 1914: 'We all know that this Civil War [threat] is a pure bogey, the Orangemen have no notion of becoming soldiers and risking their industries being killed but you always rightly maintained that the Englishman was a coward and the Orange bluff has frightened him with the result that it looks now as if the Carsonites can make their own terms instead of the Irish Party making theirs. It is pitiable after all our jubilations, all our booming of our friends the Liberals. It is the same old story, the old hatred of the Catholic.'[26]

The Irish Volunteers were an unashamedly military organization, training up an army to fight for nationalist Ireland. Thousands of young men signed up that first night; up to 5,000 more could not fit into the hall, and were signed up the following day. Among those who joined immediately was young Edward Daly, Kathleen's only brother, aged 22, fulfilling a lifetime's ambition to be a soldier. Revolutionary fervour swept the country. According to Eamonn Dore (or de hÓir) – a Volunteer who later married Kathleen's sister Nora. 'In our town [Glin, County Limerick] most of the young and old joined for to many it was a sensation and in this pre-war period everything new ... was an adventure of the first magnitude. Many ex-British soldiers were members and most of those attending drill would never have done so if they remotely knew what was at the back of the minds of those few controlling revolutioners'.[27]

The IRB intended to control the Volunteers, as secretly as possible. At a meeting in May 1914, Clarke 'was not pleased with the fact that the IRB members of the Volunteers were

not forging to the front and getting to be section leaders and
company commanders in the Volunteers. The IRB men were
to be pushed into these posts right away'.[28] But many of the
IRB men might not have been natural officers.

Early in 1914 a women's auxiliary force, Cumann na mBan,
was also established. Kathleen Clarke was a leader in the Central Branch in Dublin. While the men drilled and learnt how
to handle rifles (or at any rate broomhandles and anything
else they could find), and were given instruction in strategy
and tactics, the women also learned to handle guns, and were
given classes in bandage-making and First Aid. Meanwhile the
Fianna were being trained in street-fighting by James Connolly of the ICA: 'He had evidently made a very careful and
thorough study of the fighting that had taken place in other
countries in Europe, in Russia, and had a very thorough practical knowledge of what was required to neutralise the effect
of modern equipment and regular army troops'.[29]

Membership of the Irish Volunteers began at about
3,000, but by the following May numbers had swelled to
more than 100,000. This worried Redmond and the IPP,
and they decided to exercise full control over the growing
army. Redmond was suspicious that the IRB was influencing it, and could perhaps use such a large force to oppose the
Home Rule bill. Clarke wrote to John Daly in this regard
in April 1914, advising him that Redmond was threatening
to establish a boys' organisation as a rival to the Volunteers,

and that Joseph Devlin, another leading member of the IPP, had expressed concern that the magnetic attraction of the Volunteers to young men drew them away from the IPP.[30] In June Redmond published an ultimatum in the press, and the Volunteer Executive agreed to add twenty-five IPP nominees to its membership.

This move was supported, probably reluctantly, by Bulmer Hobson, Eoin MacNeill and Roger Casement, because they were afraid of a split in the movement. However, it was seen as the utmost treachery by the IRB; Hobson was court-martialled by it, and resigned his seat on the Supreme Council. Clarke never spoke to him again, and lost one of the few close friends he had. Indeed, Hobson had been close to all the Clarke family, and would read bedtime stories to young Daly when he was ill.[31] Denis McCullough says, 'Tom Clarke, who was a man of a very simple mind, loved and admired Hobson immensely ... the rift was very bitter and Tom would not forgive him or trust him again'.[32] Clarke and others had felt that if a split was going to come eventually, it should be sooner rather than later, and that this half-way compromise was only postponing the inevitable.

Writing much later, Hobson gave his side of the Executive affair: '[Clarke and MacDermott] were both deeply sincere men, completely devoted to the national cause; but were both narrow partisans, inclined to distrust anybody who was not a member of our small organisation. They were very suspicious of my co-operation with men like MacNeill and Casement who belonged intellectually and socially to a different world. Clarke told me about that time that he was sure Casement was a British spy.'[33] Hobson felt strongly that any move towards a rising would be a bad mistake; when James Connolly asserted that Ireland was a powder magazine and only needed someone to apply the match, Hobson replied that 'if he must talk in metaphors, Ireland was a wet bog and that the match would fall into a puddle'.[34]

MacNeill was apologetic about the Executive vote, but insisted that he had only been following Hobson's lead, and thought that Hobson was speaking for the IRB. He was not an IRB member himself. Clarke then informed MacNeill that he was not to give the oration at the upcoming Wolfe Tone commemoration at Bodenstown, as had been arranged. Clarke himself gave the oration, 'a thing he disliked, for he said he was no orator', says his wife. In his speech he said, 'The time for speaking was rapidly passing (cheers), the drilling and the arming of the people of Ireland was going to count, and was going to be the determining factor as to just how their nationalist ambition was going to be fulfilled'.[35]

To speak of drilling and arming was all very well, but there were as yet very few arms available to the Volunteers – some were even drilling with pikes, like the United Irishmen of 1798. Up north, the UVF had masterminded an illegal landing of arms and ammunition at Larne and other ports on 14

April, 1914, to public acclaim and a governmental blind eye. Ironically, considering the impending international conflict, the guns were German. The Irish Volunteers decided to do the same, also using German sources, and landed 900 guns and 26, 000 rounds of ammunition in Howth, County Dublin on 26 July 1914, with more arriving a week later in Kilcoole, County Wicklow.

The IRB members had stayed away from the Howth landing, leaving it to the Volunteers and the Fianna to collect the guns and put them in hiding, but when they realised that British army troops seemed to be heading north out of Dublin for Howth, Clarke and MacDiarmada hired cabs and went out to help. One of the first guns landed was kept by Clarke and later brought down to Limerick and presented to John Daly. Confronted by the British troops, Volunteer officers engaged them in argument, while the men behind them melted away from the road and left the rifles where they could.

Seamus Daly recalled, 'One man carrying eight rifles shouted out to me, "You'll find four more in that ditch, I cannot carry any more". We dumped the rifles in various houses and cottages.'[36] Some British troops, frustrated by the successful landing and jeered at by passers-by on the Dublin quays, fired on them, killing three and injuring nearly forty. The funerals provided another opportunity for displays of nationalist feeling.

Clarke was entitled to feel that the movement was on the up and up, but the necessary final jigsaw piece, the distraction of Britain, was not yet in place. Splits were becoming more evident in the Volunteer leadership; writing to John Devoy in August 1914, Pearse complained of MacNeill that he always bowed to the will of the Redmondites:'He is weak, hopelessly weak'.[37] Clarke himself was feeling the strain; he wrote to John Devoy, 'old age appears to be creeping on me. Most of the time I feel "moidered" and can't cope with all the work that is crying out to be attended to on my doorstep. But I'll peg away in any case....'[38]

Clarke was very careful of the Volunteers, and did not allow them to take any unnecessary risks. When Robert Brennan, a Wexford Volunteer (later Irish Ambassador to the USA) was enticed to act as a spy, he discussed it with Tom Clarke. Brennan was willing to work as a double agent, but Clarke worried that it might become known in later years, 'and all the water in the sea would not wash you clean'. He refused to allow Brennan to risk his reputation:'He took me by the collar of the coat and glared at me, saying "Drop it!" Then he gripped me by the hand and gave me one of his rare smiles. "We'll beat them without that", he said'.[39]

In August 1914, Britain declared war on Germany, and the Great War (later the First World War) began. This was the opportunity which Clarke had been hoping for all his adult life. If Ireland did not move now, it would be damned forever. His hopes were immediately dashed, however, by the long-threatened split in the Volunteers. Redmond and the IPP supported the British war effort, and a speech by Redmond at Woodenbridge, County Wicklow, on 20 September, urged the young, trained men of the Irish Volunteers to join the British Army and fight the Hun. The vast majority, to be known as the National Volunteers, did follow Redmond's lead; Éamonn de hÓir says, 'Our company…ceased to exist…the local people being 99% Redmondites'.[40]

Chapter Five
. . . . . .

16 LIVES: THOMAS CLARKE
the event of conscrip...
Diarmada, 2 T...
Co...

Planning a Rebellion
1914-15

The IRB found itself left with a rump of about 11,000 men, from a high point of 180,000 – a devastating blow to Clarke, who must have had great plans for the huge organisation he had watched develop. Desmond FitzGerald expressed this shock clearly: 'Our dream castles toppled about us with a crash. If Irishmen had served England in previous wars in their thousands, it was clear that in this war they would serve her in their tens of thousands...Our national identity was obliterated not only politically, but also in our own minds. The Irish people had recognized themselves as part of England'.[1]

Nothing daunted, the Supreme Council began to lay plans for a country-wide rebellion. Three possibilities were envisaged for setting it off – a German landing, an attempt to impose conscription on Ireland, or an imminent end to the war. Pearse drew up plans to deploy the Irish Volunteers in

...tion, encouraged by Clarke and Mac-
...here was a heated meeting of the Supreme
...cil in late September 1914, when Clarke threatened to
resign over the question of how to use the Volunteers. The
Council agreed that action should be taken before the end
of the war.

No-one knew how long the war would last. The IRB did
not want to go off half-cocked, and the preparations were
very careful, all the time under the pressure of wondering
when the war would end, and Britain turn its attention to
Ireland again. Britain, in fact, was not paying any attention
to Ireland; it was involved in a huge international struggle,
and its whole future was at stake. Ireland, even with the emotional threats from Ulster, was a footnote. The war cabinet
was a coalition of Liberals and Conservatives, who had to
work together; they were not going to rock the boat by dis-
cussing Home Rule. If they had to, they would compromise,
and that would mean partition. It was safer to park the issue
for the moment.[3]

The outbreak of war caused difficulties for American support for separatism, and many nationalist Irishmen found
themselves torn. PJ Collins, the County Cork solicitor, writing to Cohalan, who supported Germany, was trenchant in
his disagreement with this position: 'I fancy the time has
come when we can do without the Yankee dollars, this small
measure of what is called Home Rule will compel us to be

more self-reliant and I think we will make the most we can out of our own country and work out our own ideas and ideals, that is if the madman from Germany will not capture us. Honestly I prefer to be ruled by England any day than Germany, and I don't at all agree with you that Germany does not want this country. She does want it to capture the American trade and traffic'.[4]

The IRB was greatly helped by the extent of Irish anger when the Home Rule Act, signed into law on 18 September 1914, was suspended for the duration of the war. Redmond agreed to suspend Home Rule, and Asquith and the Ulster unionists agreed to suspend discussion of partition.[5] This looked like a betrayal, and played into the hands of the IRB. Britain of course needed the full support of Ulster and its heavy industry to equip its army and navy, and the suspension could be seen as a capitulation to Ulster unionism. The prime minister, Herbert Asquith, had continually sought to postpone a decision on Ulster 'exclusion' from the Home Rule bill. As the historian Ronan Fanning puts it, 'Such exercises in political Micawberism were ill suited to Ireland where they had a cumulatively devastating effect on the power base of the IPP, whose supporters ultimately deserted them in droves when the third Home Rule bill never came into effect'.[6]

The outbreak of war naturally increased pressure on the DMP and RIC to keep an eye on 'subversive elements', and

G-men, the DMP's intelligence service, rented a room across from Clarke's shop in Parnell Street to watch the comings and goings. The Daly household in Limerick was also put under surveillance. Clarke's name was placed on a 'Special War B List', and he was described as having a 'sallow complexion, dark eyes, thin visage and nose, hair and moustache dark (turning grey), abscess mark on right jaw'. He was also noted as having a 'dazed look, owing to bad sight'.[7] From November 1914 his correspondence was censored, along with that of John Daly and Seán MacDiarmada. However, none of these writers ever sent anything of importance through the ordinary mail, and the censorship was soon lifted as a waste of time.

Robert Brennan recalls a meeting of the Leinster council of the IRB in late 1914, which dealt with the problem of evading official detection. Up to that time, Brennan says, 'the Gmen had been treated as more or less of a joke... [but] so efficient were they that later, at my courtmartial, they had records to show every time I visited Tom Clarke's shop during the previous three years'. He adds, 'Tom's talk had much to do with these Gmen. We were not to let them follow us any more ...The rest of his talk had to do with discipline, being prepared, getting guns and learning to shoot. "The old enemy is in the toils", he said, "We'll get our chance now"'.[8]

Nationalist newspapers were published, each one following

the next as censorship closed them down, and often funded by the Daly family. Drilling and route marches continued in every region, as strictly as if the men were in the British army, and indeed mainly according to British army manuals; drill books could be ordered from Gale and Polden, Wellington Works, Aldershot.[9] Arms continued to be sourced; these often came from British army barracks when soldiers, in search of money for drink, would smuggle out what they could and sell it on to Volunteers. Volunteer Liam Ó Briain recalled: 'I have seen a lad come into our drill-hall displaying a brand new service rifle, and grumbling that he had had to pay half-a-crown (two shillings and six pence) for it, while a friend had got his for two shillings!'[10]

Funding was also coming from Clan na Gael, and by August 1915 more than $136,000 was lodged in a Volunteer bank account in New York.[11] Patrick McCartan returned from a trip to New York with £2000 in gold, as well as £700 in gold for Pearse's school.[12] And training continued, drawing on the lessons of what was happening in France. The *Irish Volunteer,* the official paper of the Volunteer movement, included instructions in military tactics, though the writers (sometimes including Pearse) wrote as if the Volunteers were a fully formed and professional army rather than the collection of amateurs they actually were. The paper encouraged readers to buy a copy of the London *Times* in early 1916, which included a supplement bearing Sir Ian Hamilton's full report on the battle of Gallipoli. 'Never again…will any officer be able to get so valuable a textbook for a penny'.[13]

Cumann na mBan had split as well, of course, and Kathleen Clarke continued to run the Central Branch in Dublin. To make up for the loss through censorship of various nationalist newspapers, she had the idea of publishing pamphlets on Irish revolutionaries throughout history, to be sold at 1p each. They sold in their thousands; the first one was written by Pearse, on Wolfe Tone. According to Kathleen's memoir, Cumann na mBan also 'ran classes in first aid, signalling and rifle practice, lessons in cleaning and loading rifles and small arms … held whist drives, ceilidh (dances) or anything which would make money for the purpose [of equipping the Volunteers]'.[14]

With both Tom and herself so busy, babysitting became a concern when she had to attend Central Branch lectures. She describes an evening when she had to leave the three boys alone, even though she knew that Emmet, the youngest, 'had a passion for fire and was rather wild'. However, she decided to leave them to God, had a serious chat with them about their duty to Ireland, and went. 'When I arrived home some hours later I found they had kept their word. I was very proud of them and hugged them and gave them a lovely supper.'[15] Housekeeping standards also slipped, and her sisters were inclined to be critical on their visits, and to complain that she slapped her children too much. This must have irritated her intensely; she and her husband were running two shops and rearing three children on a low income, with little domestic help.

Kathleen became increasingly annoyed at the 'jingoism' of the calls for Irishmen to join the British army, as large numbers were doing. Hundreds of people walked past the shop every day wearing the Union Jack on their lapels. She decided to counter the imperialist propaganda by creating a nationalist symbol which people could wear. While in New York, she had observed Clan na Gael badges made of green, white and orange ribbons, so she used these as a template and began to sell similar badges over the counter in the shop, at a penny each. She sold out the first hundred in a day, and continued to make them with the help of the Irish Citizen Army, in Liberty Hall.[16]

Roger Casement, a civil servant member of the Volunteer Executive who had fundraised for arms, decided to make contact with prisoners-of-war in Germany and raise an Irish Brigade to help. He did not discuss his plan with the IRB or the Volunteers, and Clarke was angry at this solo run; the IRB had not wanted German help, apart from the guns. He read Casement's plan to the Supreme Council, said 'Now you have all heard this and you understand what is in it, so we will destroy it', and immediately put a match to it.[17] When Clan na Gael in America endorsed Casement's plan, Clarke reluctantly agreed to it, but sent Captain Robert

Monteith off to follow Casement and provide help and advice. Monteith, who had been employed in the Ordnance Department at Islandbridge, had lost his job because he acted as a military instructor for the Volunteers, and was under sentence of deportation. 'Tom decided to give him £100 for his expenses; this sum was handed to him in Tom's shop', says Diarmuid Lynch, a member of the IRB Executive.[18]

Casement failed to raise an Irish brigade, but he did conclude a treaty with the Germans; a copy was published in the *Gaelic American*, with the seal of the Imperial German Government. Among other things, it promised that if the Irish Brigade could not be used in Ireland, it could instead help to drive the British out of Egypt. Casement's initiative had very little support in Ireland.

In May 1915, the Clarkes' eldest son Daly, now aged 13, started to attend Pearse's school, St Enda's, Rathfarnham, and seems to have settled down well there. His fees were probably paid by the Daly family.

Seán MacDiarmada was arrested in June for making a seditious speech in Tuam, County Galway. He was visited by Kathleen Clarke while in Arbour Hill barracks after his arrest, and by Tom Clarke in Mountjoy Jail, where he was sentenced to four months' imprisonment. Writing to John Daly, Seán professes himself a changed man, with no smoking or drinking or reading in bed: 'I miss my little game of bridge, but oh couldn't I do justice to a good cigar now…'.[19]

A note in *The Irish Volunteer,* edited by Eoin MacNeill, announced: 'Seán MacDiarmada is not in the prison hospital or receiving any special favours in his prison treatment. He is doing hard labour, and is as happy in mind as any honest Irishman can be, while the day of Irish freedom is delayed'.

Irish Freedom had by now been suppressed, so Clarke launched *Nationality*, a weekly publication edited by Arthur Griffith, on 26 June. Griffith was under strict instructions to toe the republican editorial line, but MacDiarmada disapproved of him being given this responsibility, not trusting him.

The next set-piece nationalist demonstration arose from the death in New York, aged 83, of that recalcitrant Fenian Jeremiah O'Donovan Rossa, the original author of the dynamite campaign. Devoy cabled the news to Clarke, seeking instructions about using this opportunity, and Clarke said to his wife, 'If Rossa had planned to die at the most opportune time for serving his country, he could not have done better'.[20] O'Donovan Rossa had wished to be brought back to Ireland for burial, and Clarke saw a glorious opportunity for a peaceful but important public declaration of nationalist feeling.

Committees were established and plans set in train. Clarke was the main mover in all of this; Seán McGarry said later, 'During the few weeks preceding the funeral his [Clarke's] energy seemed to be inexhaustible and the plans for the route and the dispositions of the various participating bodies which appeared in the papers were actually drawn by himself on the counter in his shop'.[21] John Devoy sent £20 to buy the grave.[22] Rossa's wife and daughter accompanied the remains, and were greeted in Liverpool by Kathleen Clarke and Seán McGarry, who were to escort them to Dublin. Clarke had warned Kathleen that if she was asked her nationality she was to say 'British', in case she would be delayed; she remembered, 'It was a hard thing for me to do, and the recollection of it still hurts'.[23]

O'Donovan Rossa's body arrived in Dublin on 26 July, and was brought first to the Pro-Cathedral in Dublin for a night (after an argument with the Archbishop), then to City Hall, where it lay in state till Sunday 1 August. The funeral arrangements had been made under the auspices of the Wolfe Tone Memorial Association, a 'front' name which the IRB often used. On the Sunday, an immense procession moved off from City Hall to Glasnevin Cemetery; the First Battalion of the Volunteers, under Kathleen's brother Edward Daly, now a Commandant, provided the guard of honour.

At Glasnevin, the graveside oration was given by Patrick Pearse. When he had asked Clarke how far he could go, Clarke had insisted, 'Make it as hot as hell, throw discretion to the winds'. Pearse certainly lived up to this advice, and his speech at this funeral has gone down as one of the most eloquent appeals to nationalist sentiment in recent Irish history. In his peroration, he declaimed: 'The defenders of this

Realm have worked well in secret and in the open ... they think that they have foreseen everything, think that they have provided against everything; but the fools, the fools, the fools! – they have left us our Fenian dead, and while Ireland holds these graves, Ireland unfree shall never be at peace'.

There was an intense silence, followed by wave after wave of cheers. In the following weeks, the ranks of the Volunteers and Cumann na mBan swelled further. MacDiarmada apparently later complained to Clarke that Pearse had 'no right to reach out and grasp the honour due to others'. Clarke replied, 'Sure it doesn't matter who gets the glory so long as the things are being done'.[24]

In September, MacDiarmada was released from prison. He was collected by the Clarkes and brought to their home, now in Richmond Avenue, Fairview. He and Clarke argued about the future of the Gaelic League; IRB infiltration had gradually given it a more political flavour, causing the resignation of founder members such as Douglas Hyde. Thomas Ashe once described the IRB plan as 'to rid it of some of the old women and some of the fossils that control it at present'.[25] Seán feared the League would wither, and that the IRB would be blamed for its loss. Clarke argued that it could not fail; its work was too important, and the country needed to have its language restored to it.[26] Although Clarke and Kathleen professed a sentimental attachment to the preservation of the language, neither of them spoke Irish, as it had not been part of their backgrounds or education. Indeed, a member of the Gaelic League had verbally attacked Kathleen in the shop one day for not speaking Irish, and her husband had had to write a strong letter in her defence.[27]

Clarke was still to all intents and purposes a quiet shop-keeper, and never let this mask slip in front of anyone he did not know, as various hopeful young people found. William Daly from London, visiting the shop, tried to give Clarke a rifle which he had smuggled over from England, but Clarke, suspicious of his cockney accent, told him to take himself and his rifle 'away to hell from him'.[28] Sydney Gifford, who had a rather English accent, tried to engage him in con-versation about nationalism, 'but he shut up and assumed a real business manner. He obviously thought that I was prob-ably sent by Dublin Castle to extract some information from him'. When he later wished to talk to her about an article she had written, she at first refused to meet 'that old crank', but they became friends. When his 'Prison Diary' was pub-lished (it was serialised in *Irish Freedom*, 1912-13), she asked him jokingly whether the author was a relation of his: 'He said, "it is me". He never talked about his prison experiences except when a question was put to him'.[29]

Arms were still being collected.; Joseph O'Rourke recalls, 'During the winter of 1915 we were getting in several cargoes of arms ... Tom Clarke paid for [one] by writing an order to Mrs Clarke on a paper snuffbag, which I duly presented to

Mrs Clarke in Richmond Road. She asked me would it be ok in cash and gave me between £500 or £600…'[30] A scribbled list of accounts, among the Clarke Papers in the NLI, shows the money that was being spent on arms and equipment: '17 Martini rifles, £38.5.0; 10,000 x .303 [ammunition], £60.0.0; 1 heliograph, £1.5.0…'[31]

Clearly, large sums passed through the hands of the Clarkes, but they rigorously kept this money separate from their own funds; their children went to national schools, and references to worn-out shoes and shabby shirts in Kathleen's letters indicate that they lived strictly within their means. Any large expense, such as Daly's fees at Pearse's school, was covered by the Daly family, but Kathleen was always very reluctant to ask her sister Madge for help.

The Supreme Council by now had given organisational responsibility to its Executive, essentially Clarke and Mac-Diarmada. These two had an advisory committee of Commandants and Vice-commandants who were also in the IRB (not all of them were), but Clarke decided this was too large, and dissolved it. In early 1915 he passed its recommendations to a smaller group, consisting of Patrick Pearse, Joseph Plunkett (Director of Operations of the Volunteers), and Éamonn Ceannt, a Sinn Féin and Gaelic League member, in early 1915. At the end of May he upgraded this trio to a formal Military Council; the Supreme Council only learned of its existence some time later, and was never kept informed of its activities.

Clarke and MacDiarmada joined this Military Council in September 1915. They then gained complete control of the Supreme Council in December by engineering the election of Denis McCullough as chairman: as he was based in Belfast, and rarely able to attend Dublin meetings, he could effectively be by-passed. They had specifically blocked Pearse from being chairman; MacDiarmada had said to McCullough, 'Sure we couldn't control the bloody man', and McCullough himself felt that Pearse was 'up in the clouds'.[32]

Plunkett had devised a military strategy which he had worked on for some years, and it was adopted by the Military Council without any changes. It centred on a rising in Dublin, supported by troops from Germany – Plunkett apparently envisaged 12,000 German troops, bringing with them 40,000 rifles. The Military Council thought highly of his military expertise. They were in fact preparing to join Turkey and Bulgaria, allying with the Central Powers against the Allies. They were all fascinated by the progress of the war, and followed it in detail, convinced of a German victory.

WJ McCormack mentions that international trends may have influenced the Military Council, even though the rising was predominantly driven by an Irish national tradition. 'The leaders … were certainly conscious of intellectual developments elsewhere, and nowhere is that more clearly evident than in the pages of the *Irish Review*'. Founded in 1911 as a literary review, many of the *Irish Review* articles were writ-

ten by the 'intellectuals' in the IRB leadership – MacDonagh, Pearse, Plunkett, Connolly, Willie Pearse, each of whom
was a poet, playwright, editor or teacher, or a combination
of these. Several of these writers were ultimately signatories
of the Proclamation. Plunkett became owner and editor of
the *Irish Review* in 1913.[33] Despite the best efforts of Connolly, none of these 'intellectuals' was interested in socialism.
McCormack adds, 'Tom Clarke, Seán Heuston, Seán Mac-
Diarmada and John MacBride were *not* intellectuals.'

The decision to mount a rebellion came as a surprise to
Clan na Gael in New York. They had thought that the war
situation was not favourable enough, but the Military Council in Dublin insisted that the situation was more propitious
now than it might be later. It did not ask Clan na Gael for
advice, but presented them with a *fait accompli*. Clan na Gael,
accepting the authority of the Dublin leadership, decided
that its duty was to give all the help possible.[34] David Thornley, a later commentator, wrote: 'To no single figure, Clarke,
Pearse or MacDiarmada, can the inspiration of 1916 be
ascribed. But undoubtedly the fact that Clarke, the symbolic
fellow-martyr of an older generation, was prepared to throw
the weight of his name behind the young men and their
policy of action was a major policy in its success.'[35] However,
it seems to have been Clarke himself who pushed the policy
of action, and guided the younger men towards it.

Three main factors motivated Clarke. He feared the war

would end soon, and that there would be a peace conference without Irish representation. He felt that the Irish people were too inert, and had to be roused by violent rebellion. Finally, it was plain that the Volunteers would soon become demoralised by constant drilling without any real action, particularly when massive battles were raging in France. Already they were being jeered at in the streets as 'toy soldiers'. In fact, about three weeks before the rising there was a clash in Tullamore, County Offaly, between Volunteers and members of the RIC, which greatly annoyed Clarke and MacDiarmada.[36] It was time to give the troops something to do.

The Clarke family spent Christmas 1915 at the Daly home in Limerick, along with Ned Daly, Ned's best friend Captain James O'Sullivan (later to marry Laura Daly), Con Colbert (a Volunteer from County Limerick) and Seán MacDiarmada. It was a convivial gathering, and ended a busy year for Tom Clarke. He and his family returned to Dublin, to what was to be their last few months together.

Many of the men who died in the Rising left young wives and families behind them, and it is not always clear that their wives and children had known what to expect. In Clarke's family, this was not a question; Kathleen knew well what was to happen, and seems to have accepted the necessity – not without concern, as she looked at her young sons, but well aware that this was her husband's life's ambition, and she could not (and would not) hold him back from it.

Undoubtedly Clarke had to overcome many feelings of weakness as he looked forward to the Rising, and the risk that he might not survive it. He was obviously a very devoted husband, and seems also to have been a loving and attentive father, keen to spend time with his sons and to encourage them in their interests, in the brief times when he was neither in the shop nor engaged in endless meetings and committees. The sons seem to have been very attached to their father, and glad to spend whatever time they could with him.

From the early letters Kathleen wrote from Limerick to Tom in Dublin, when Daly was six, the affection is very clear: '[Daly] gives me lots of kisses every day to send to papa and is always asking when am I going to take him up to you'.[37] Tom was good at writing funny stories for the child which made him laugh. One undated letter promises him a new friendship: 'Granny Clarke has a big black dog with a bushy tail. His name is Kruger because he does not like the English. He is a great dog and always wants to carry a parcel in his mouth when he is going out ... When you come to Dublin I am going to make him your friend'. In May he wrote, 'tell Daly I'm lonely and I have no one to send out to get the good apples for me'.

Kathleen was aware of a father's influence: 'He is no easy child to manage, he is so sharp and his will so strong, when you come down I'd like you'd be more loving to him, as

I believe he is more easily influenced that way than being abused'.[38]

She gives her husband all the details any devoted father would want, obviously knowing he would be interested: 'The baby [Tom] I find is a music lover, as soon as he hears singing or any kind of music he gets quiet, no matter how restless he is … Daly has taken to singing lately, and it would make you roar to hear himself and Mama singing duets. Kitty of Coleraine is his favourite …' (Tom replied that Daly might have the ear, but 'he is like his dad, not for to save his neck could he sing an air correctly'). She also points out that the baby was very like Daly, 'only his hair is brown and grows down in a peak almost on top, like yours did when you had it'.[39]

Young Daly was delighted at the thought of seeing his father again in Dublin, although he was happy in Limerick: 'He is out every day on the street and is as well known as a bad penny in William St, and is generally set down as an odd child, one not able to be bought or coaxed or frightened … He won't play with any boy, big or small, unless he is boss'.[40]

When Tom himself was in Limerick with young Tom (then aged four), he found he could manage the child well: 'certainly my being here has a large influence with him in keeping him from kicking up – a word from me, should he be disposed to kick up, always puts him right at once. He sleeps with me and keeps as quiet as a mouse until I wake'.[41] Emmet, the youngest, was a different kettle of fish: 'God

almighty what an obstreperous kid I discovered Emmet to
be when I was at close quarters with him for the two days [of
Christmas]', Tom wrote to John Daly in 1911, adding, 'Daly
full of excitement and big words over his Santa Claus toys
which include a hammer (and said hammer can bang!)'.[42]

In an account Kathleen wrote years later, she said of Tom:
'He adored his children and was never happier than when
playing with them. Emmet's artlessness was a continuous
delight to him. He was very proud of Daly's cleverness, and
Tom's ability to get out of scrapes (he was always in them)
was another source of amusement to him'.[43]

Baby Tom had stayed in Limerick for quite some time
after his birth. Kathleen was trying to organise a home in
Dublin, then Tom senior had contracted typhoid. Mrs Daly
was deeply attached to the child, particularly after Annie's
death, and was very unwilling to let him go back to his
mother, though Kathleen repeatedly requested it. His brother
Emmet remembered: 'When Tom was naughty his aunts used
threaten to send him to his mother in Dublin; so he came
to Dublin with a certain fear of his mother. Finally, Uncle
John insisted that Tom go to Dublin or he would grow up
a spoilt brat.'[44] The child must have been well over a year
old by the time the family was reunited, and even then his
granny stayed with them in Dublin for six weeks before let-
ting him go.

Tom Clarke's youngest son Emmet was interviewed for

radio by Donncha Ó Dulaing in April 1991. Then aged 81, Emmet had only been six when his father died, but had some surprisingly clear memories, and the interview is very emotional. He portrays a father who was interested in everything, would explain things clearly and patiently, and was always keen to help his sons' education, for example collecting leaves on the street when they needed to bring some into school. Emmet described him as 'a very good father', but equally agreed that his whole attention was on Ireland.[45]

Emmet admits that his memories are only a child's memories, but none of them were bad. He remembered no fights or arguments, they were a happy family. Tom Clarke himself set in motion the events which would demolish this happiness, for what he saw as a higher end. Kathleen should perhaps have the last word here: 'Except for the lack of worldly goods, the marriage was ideally happy, so happy that he was often haunted by the fear that it was too great to last … looking back it seems strange that the one thing he feared, he helped to bring about'.[46]

Chapter Six

• • • • • •

The Easter Rising

From the turn of the twentieth century, events had been moving quickly in both nationalist and labour movements. Founded in 1909 by James Larkin, the Irish Transport and General Workers Union (ITGWU) had begun recruiting carters and labourers, and when employers reacted aggressively to this, Dublin was hit by a massive strike in 1913, 'The Dublin Lockout'. Union leaders included James Connolly, a Scottish socialist and union organiser, who had been Belfast organiser for the ITGWU for a time, and had come to Dublin to help with the Lockout. When the Employers' Federation insisted on written undertakings from their workers that they would not join a union on pain of dismissal, 700 out of the Dublin tram company's 1700 workers came out on strike, and thousands more, such as the coal workers, were locked out for supporting them.

By September 1913, 25,000 workers were out of work, and their families were suffering; without a social welfare system, they were dependent on private charity, and the unions' rapidly-depleting funds. As conditions worsened, Jim Larkin, the ITGWU leader, called on British dock workers to come out in sympathy, but the British TUC refused to back this call, and the strike collapsed. The Dublin Lockout finally ended in February 1914; the men had been driven back to work by hunger, and the needs of their families. Throughout, Tom Clarke had marked his support for the strikers by refusing to stock the *Irish Independent*, owned by one of the strongest employers, William Martin Murphy, 'in spite of all the pressure that powerful corporation was able to concentrate upon him'.[1]

The strike was marked by several bloody confrontations between strikers, blacklegs and police; the police, in particular the Dublin Metropolitan Police (DMP), were later accused of losing control and beating anyone in their path. Despite his desire for a low profile, Clarke was sufficiently horrified to write a two-page letter condemning police brutality which was published in *Irish Freedom* and *The Irish Worker*. In it, he harks back to his youth: 'I ... was present when buckshot in volleys was fired into an unarmed crowd in Dungannon, which so infuriated them that in their frenzy they closed in on a strong posse of police who were sweeping through them with fixed bayonets ... and put them to flight. I saw brutal things done that day on both sides ... Later on I witnessed the Bowery hooligans and New York

police have a "set to". The fight was fierce and some savage acts were witnessed. It has fallen to my lot to get considerable first hand knowledge of the ruffianism of the criminal classes of London's underworld. Yet nothing I know of during my whole career can match the downright inhuman savagery that was witnessed recently in the [Dublin] streets ... when the police were let loose to run amok and indiscriminately bludgeon every man, woman and child they came across...'
His letter called for an independent public enquiry.[2]

Connolly, greatly angered by the employers' intransigence, and by the aggressive tactics of the police, decided to help workers to defend themselves. In November 1913, he gathered men together, and under the command of Jack White, ex-British Army, the Irish Citizen Army learned to drill and parade. This was partly to give the unemployed something to do, but it also enabled them to protect union meetings, although they were armed only with hurleys. After the Lockout ended, Connolly took the remaining 200 or so men, and reorganised the Irish Citizen Army into a revolutionary force. Its headquarters were in Liberty Hall, HQ of the ITGWU. Its two aims, as laid down by Connolly, were the ownership of the land of Ireland by the people of Ireland, and the establishment of a 'Workers' Republic'.

Connolly was more a socialist than a republican, but he saw the worth of collaborating with the Irish Volunteers. However, relations began badly when ICA members were

thrown out of the meeting which saw the founding of the
Volunteers. The ICA members were disrupting the meeting because of the presence of Tom Kettle, once of the IPP,
on the platform, because his family had locked out workers.
However, after the outbreak of war in 1914, the two organisations moved closer together. Connolly in fact was inclined
to feel that the Volunteers were afraid to commit themselves
to a proper revolution. In July 1915, Seán McGarry asked
Connolly to write for the souvenir booklet produced for
O'Donovan Rossa's funeral, and Connolly burst out, 'When
are you fellows going to stop blethering about *dead* Fenians?
Why don't you get a few *live* ones for a change?' Tom Clarke
said, 'Send him to me. I'll fix that', and Connolly, having met
Clarke, wrote an article 'in which he managed to turn a dead
Fenian into a live incitement to revolution'.[3]

Connolly was a far more impetuous man than Clarke, and
felt that the IRB was dragging its feet. Detailed planning was
all very well, but if the war suddenly ended, this great chance
would have been missed. His newspaper, the *Workers' Republic*, became more and more belligerent through 1914 and
1915, almost talking openly of revolution, and the Supreme
Council became worried. As McGarry recalled, 'He [Con-
nolly] wanted to shout it from the housetops, did not care
how soon it started or with how many men. He believed
that once the standard of revolt was raised the people – his
people – would rally to it and he was afraid of a sudden

collapse of the war … Tom, who had infinite patience in a matter of this kind, had his hands full'.[4]

In early January 1916, the Irish Citizen Army began to practise manoeuvres at night around Dublin Castle, and the authorities became alarmed. Shortly afterwards a document smuggled out of Dublin Castle, where the intelligence services were based, urged instant arrest of the ICA leaders. This was too close for comfort. Seán T Ó Ceallaigh and Diarmuid Lynch hurried down to Limerick, where Clarke and Mac-Diarmada were spending a few days with the Dalys, to discuss the matter. It would seem that arrangements were made to meet Connolly, and persuade him to pull back from his inflammatory course.[5]

Connolly spent some days in January 1916 with members of the Supreme Council, and during this time he was persuaded to hold his fire until the date they had decided, the upcoming Easter. Whether this meeting was voluntary or not is disputed. Some accounts hold that he was actually kidnapped by the IRB, others that he planned his 'disappearance' himself and had given orders to the ICA to strike if he was not back by a certain time. The truth will probably never be known; certainly Kathleen Clarke, in her memoir, depicted Clarke and Seán MacDiarmada as being completely unaware of Connolly's whereabouts, but her brother, Commandant Edward Daly, had been put on notice to bring Connolly to a meeting if he resisted.[6] Connolly himself never explained it fully to anyone. From then on the Volunteers and the ICA worked and drilled together with one aim, an armed revolution, and Connolly began to attend meetings of the Military Council.

From early 1916, events moved even more quickly, and Volunteer activity became more intense. Kathleen's brother Ned walked the streets of his command area, the Four Courts district, plotting barricades and escape routes, while supervising the movement of food supplies and ammunition into homes near to the Four Courts buildings. The other commandants were making similar plans, and the ordinary Volunteers were well aware that something big was coming, even if it was not spelt out.

In late December 1915 or early January 1916, the small, secretive Military Council fixed the date of the Rising for Easter 1916. Even the Supreme Council, meeting in Clontarf on 16 January, was not told of this decision. The Military Council simply sought agreement that the IRB would rise at the earliest possible time, and the Supreme Council assented.

Although Bulmer Hobson was a senior member of the IRB, and Eoin MacNeill was head of the Volunteers, they were sidelined completely. As Foy and Barton put it, 'they [Clarke and MacDiarmada] slowly stripped MacNeill of effective control … while IRB loyalists acquired operational control of the organisation. Hobson, for his part, was watching for incriminating evidence against his enemies and became a brooding nemesis over Clarke and MacDiarmada, forcing them and their allies to be perpetually on guard. When challenged about their activities they adopted a façade of evasion, pained indignation or simply lied'.[7]

At the January Clontarf meeting, Denis McCullough said that they would need a full-time organiser for Ulster; he himself ran his own business, had a young family and no military training, so could not do it. A Dr Harry Burke from Carrickmacross convinced the council that he could do it, and was given a motorcycle, a generous allowance, and the title 'O/C Ulster Forces of the Irish Republic'. Burke was never heard from again until he was seen in Richmond Barracks after the Rising; Clarke and MacDiarmada had trusted the wrong man. He certainly made no effort to organise anything.

The plan for the north was that a coded message was to be sent when the time came, and McCullough's Belfast Volunteers were to head for Tyrone to meet the other Ulster troops, and all would march to join Liam Mellows in Connaught. McCullough could not understand the need for this long march through enemy territory, poorly armed; could they not at least attack RIC barracks to try to get more weapons? But Connolly insisted that 'no shot is to be fired in Ulster'. Pearse smoothed things down by saying, 'If we win through, we will then deal with Ulster'. McCullough's witness statement concludes, 'I ... am fully convinced that it was not intended that any action should be taken by the Belfast group. Seán MacDiarmada, at least, knew the situation in Belfast and indeed in Ulster generally, and understood the difficulties and obstacles we were likely to encounter…'[8] The northern Volunteers were being quietly left out of the fight.

The Military Council had moved to set a date because of the probability that the authorities would not remain inert for much longer. Already the drilling of the Volunteers and the ICA activities had attracted attention. On 17 March, St Patrick's Day, 1916, the Dublin Brigade of the Irish Volunteers, almost fully armed and equipped, paraded through Dublin and stopped traffic going through Dame Street, from the City Hall to the Bank of Ireland, for over an hour. Later, marching down Manor Street, Seamus Daly remembers, 'we met a company of infantry coming down from Marlborough Barracks. Most of our men were in uniform. The street is very wide there … Just as the head of our company met theirs, the O/C of the British company gave the "eyes right" and our skipper immediately returned the compliment'. [9]

The intelligence concerns were not shared by administration in Dublin Castle, despite the increasingly despairing reports from the DMP and the RIC. Police spies and informers were aware that matters were coming to a head, but no-one in Dublin Castle was paying attention. The administration consisted of Chief Secretary Augustine Birrell, 'amiable but indolent', who had never wanted the job, and Sir

Matthew Nathan, Under-Secretary, head of the civil service. They were led by the viceroy, Lord Wimborne, who had a reputation as 'the best judge of good wine and bad women in Ireland'.[10] Birrell's view was that to try and arrest Volunteers would only cause trouble, and that there wasn't enough proper leadership for a full-scale rising; Nathan reluctantly accepted this view.

Birrell later accepted responsibility for the failure to anticipate the Rising. However, his wife had become insane from a brain tumour in 1913, and he travelled back to England frequently to visit her, so he could be forgiven for failing to see what was happening. In London, the coalition government under Asquith was refusing to decide on the position of Ulster in the Home Rule Bill, causing enormous uncertainty in Ulster and in the rest of Ireland, and should have been aware that the situation was very volatile. The government later complained that Dublin Castle had kept reassuring them that all was quiet.

Agitated reports continued to flood into the Castle. One RIC report said that the Volunteer organisation was 'well organised, governed by a thoroughly disloyal directorate, and in the way of injuring recruiting and spreading sedition, does a great deal of harm'.[11] Inspector General Chamberlain of the RIC wrote passionately, 'I submit it is now time to seriously consider whether the organizers of the IV can be allowed with safety to continue their mischievous work, and whether this Force so hostile to British interests can be permitted to increase its strength and remain any longer in possession of arms without grave danger to the state'.[12]

At the end of January, Tom Clarke suffered a gunshot wound in the arm. Seán McGarry, his aide-de-camp, had pointed a small pistol at him in fun, saying, 'It's all right, Tom, it's not loaded'. It was pointing at Clarke's heart, and as he moved aside it went off, shattering his elbow. The following morning the bullet and splinters of bone were removed in the Mater Hospital. A memoir by an anonymous nun in the hospital states that Clarke refused to go to confession and receive communion before the operation, 'which caused a certain amount of worry to us'. No record of the operation was kept; the surgeon, Denis Farnan, a nationalist sympathiser, may have feared it would lead to trouble.[13]

The injury was to Clarke's right arm, and he had to learn to use a revolver with his left hand for the Rising. He made excuses for McGarry, but Kathleen never forgave the man. MacDiarmada, hearing of the shooting, said to her, 'Did you realise if Tom was dead, all our hope of a Rising was gone?'[14] To recover, Clarke went down to the Daly home in Limerick for a few days. Kathleen preserved a souvenir of this accident; the note with it, in her handwriting, reads, 'This silk square was one worn by Thomas Clarke to support his arm after he was accidently [sic] shot in the arm on January 31st 1916. He never recovered the full use of it'.[15]

About six weeks before the Rising, all senior officers of the Volunteers who were not already in the IRB were approached, and, if agreeable, sworn into the organisation. Those who did so were then informed that only orders signed by Patrick Pearse, as commander-in-chief, were to be obeyed, i.e. that orders from MacNeill were to be ignored.[16] In February 1916, Pearse was still categorically denying to MacNeill that any Rising was planned. MacNeill himself was not opposed to the idea of a Rising, but insisted that it could only succeed with the backing of the Irish people, and preferably in response to a provocation such as conscription. He had no interest in a Rising that would be bound to fail.

On St Patrick's Day, 17 March 1916, a conference was held at Dublin Castle. Present were Major General LB Friend, GOC British forces in Ireland; Major Ivor Price, Intelligence Officer; John Gordon, the Attorney General; WA O'Connell, DIG of the RIC; and Sir Matthew Nathan, Under-Secretary. They discussed the Irish Volunteer travelling organisers, but agreed that internment was impossible without proof of hostile association. The deportation of several persons of interest was agreed. 'Reports were read with regard to TJ Clarke, ex-Fenian and convict whose shop was now the meeting place of the more violent revolutionaries and the advisability of his reincarceration under his former sentence discussed. The Attorney General was on the whole against this unless some new offence could be proved.'

Major General Friend urged that newspaper presses printing seditious material should be broken up. The meeting also discussed interference with recruiting meetings, which was widespread in some parts of the country, and whether night manoeuvres in Dublin could be prevented. The Irish Volunteers could only be proceeded against by proclaiming them an illegal organisation; this course was not recommended. After a discussion of house searches of Volunteer leaders in Cork, the conference adjourned; there seems to have been little sense of urgency.[17]

Early in April, Clarke asked Kathleen to give him a list of Cumann na mBan members who could be trusted to work as couriers, and she did so; 'I have the intense satisfaction that all were true to the trust placed in them'[18]. One of these brave messengers, Kitty O'Doherty, recalled Tom Clarke warning her that she should be ready to go to any port in Ireland at very short notice; this would have related to possible arms landings.[19]

On Saturday 15 April, Denis McCullough came down from the north to find out what was going on. He confronted Tom Clarke, but Clarke swore to him that he knew nothing except that he was to report to his brother-in-law, Commandant Edward Daly, on Easter Sunday, and follow Daly's orders. He assured McCullough that the only ones who knew what was to happen were MacDiarmada, Pearse and Connolly. McCullough believed him, but of course Clarke knew exactly what was to happen, and where.

McCullough then met MacDiarmada, who was very surprised to see him. McCullough insisted on having it out with him, and MacDiarmada revealed the plans for Dublin, the planned landing of German arms in Kerry, and the expectation of a ship coming into Dublin Bay with German officers on board. McCullough, taking all this with a grain of salt, insisted he would bring his men to Tyrone and carry out his orders, whether they were backed up or not, and that he would call MacDiarmada to account, if they both lived. 'He laughed and said that there wasn't much chance of that, if the Rising came off, so he wasn't worried at answering for his actions'.[20]

That Saturday night, the day before Palm Sunday, Bulmer Hobson spoke at an IRB meeting, camouflaged by a Cumann na mBan concert and dance, and warned against the use of physical force. He agreed that the Volunteers should continue to develop their forces, so that they might force the issue about a seat at post-war peace talks, but, he added, no man had any right to sacrifice other lives 'merely that he might make for himself a bloody niche in history'.[21] Hobson feared the direction in which the IRB was moving, but he was certain that the majority of the Volunteers would be opposed to a violent rebellion. He was confident of influencing MacNeill, later asserting, 'It was often easier to convince MacNeill that nothing could be done, than it was to spur him into positive action'. Hobson also wrote that Pearse believed in the need for a blood sacrifice: 'Pearse was full of notions drawn from the Old Testament about being the scapegoat of the people'.[22]

Con Colbert, a leading Volunteer from County Limerick, called into Clarke's shop to complain about holding a *ceilidh* on that Saturday, a day which marked the beginning of Holy Week. The hastily-arranged entertainment had been designed as a cover for men from the provinces arriving for the IRB meeting, but Kathleen could not explain that to the pious Colbert. Instead she told him that he should dance while he could, because he might be dancing at the end of a rope soon. She was shocked at herself, but confesses that she was under great strain at the time.[23]

On Palm Sunday, a meeting was held in Clontarf at which Patrick O'Daly, who had worked in the Magazine Fort in the Phoenix Park, helped to devise a plan to capture the Fort. It involved playing a football game in front of the gates, so that they could be reached without causing suspicion; some of the young lads of the Fianna would be useful for this. Thomas MacDonagh wanted to take the ammunition out of the Fort, but Clarke and MacDiarmada preferred to have the whole place blown up. Clarke said that the ammunition would be used against them if it was not destroyed. O'Daly was not aware of the planned rebellion, but certainly guessed that something big would come off soon. 'They had a discussion on the gun-cotton store and … I learned for the first time that you could burn gun-cotton without exploding it. It was Tom Clarke who said that'.[24]

On Tuesday 18 April, the Military Council held a meeting in Henry Street, at the home of Jennie Wyse Power (first president of Cumann na mBan). At this meeting, the Proclamation was read and agreed by all present. MacNeill was not there, so MacDiarmada took the Proclamation to show it to him, and persuade him to sign it. MacDiarmada apparently reported back that MacNeill had either signed or agreed to sign the Proclamation, but Kathleen's memoir is vague on that point – she was writing several decades later. Certainly, MacNeill never did sign the Proclamation. Clarke and Mac-Diarmada were to be the only civilian members of the new government, which otherwise had a strongly military flavour; Pearse, Connolly and Plunkett were to be 'commandants general'. FX Martin later described them as a 'revolutionary junta', planning a militarised state.[25]

Kathleen worried about Tom, as he had not returned home by midnight, and walked up and down the avenue looking for him. Finally she saw him, and walked to meet him: 'He seemed so joyous and excited, telling me he had great news … we talked well into the night, or rather the morning'. Clarke described the meeting and the reading of the Proclamation, and said he had been first signatory. Both he and Kathleen took this to mean that he would be President of the new republic. He had been reluctant to take on that honour, but Thomas MacDonagh had declared that he would not sign it at all unless Tom Clarke's name came first. Pearse had been designated Commander-in-Chief of Ireland, and Connolly Commander of Dublin. Tom confided that one of the signatories had been opposed to the clause about equal rights for women, and he told Kathleen who it was, but frustratingly she does not reveal that in her memoir.[26]

It is possible that the Proclamation was not actually signed in person by anyone, but that the names were listed by someone (probably Connolly) in a given order for the printers at Liberty Hall to add. The printers were directed by Connolly to destroy the original copy, so there may have been actual signatures attached to it, but the printers would have also needed a clearly-written list in order to decipher what might have been illegible signatures. Clarke, for example, with his injured right arm, could hardly have written his name clearly, and MacDonagh's handwriting was notoriously bad.[27]

Clarke told his wife about the plans for the Rising, and also discussed them with Ned Daly. Kathleen could see that Ned had had a bit of a shock; he had known a Rising would take place, but not so soon. There was going to be a busy week of preparation. Sometime previously, Kathleen had been taken into the confidence of the IRB; if they all died during the Rising, someone would have to continue the struggle, and no-one could be better trusted than she. She was to be entrusted with money for the dependants of men killed or injured in the fighting. Hopes were high; there were at most 25,000 British troops in Ireland, many of them untried recruits, and their barracks were full of weapons which could be captured. If the rebels could hold out for a few months, the Irish-Americans would probably come to their aid.

Kathleen listened to Tom's excited plans with a sinking heart. She had always expected this day would come, but did not believe the plans could succeed. 'It seemed to me the odds were too great, and as far as I was concerned I could see my happiness at an end. I felt Tom would not come through, and I think he knew he would not, but neither of us would admit it.'[28]

Meanwhile, Sir Roger Casement's German contacts had borne fruit. A ship called the *Aud* was on its way from Germany to County Kerry, with a cargo of 20,000 weapons, organised with the help of Clan na Gael. Casement, however, believed that this was inadequate, and sent an urgent message to the IRB in Dublin telling them to delay the Rising, that it had no hope of success. On Good Friday he landed at Banna Strand, County Kerry, from a German U-boat, and was arrested. British sources had been warned of the German arms delivery, and were on the look-out.

The *Aud* had no wireless, so did not know that the date of the Rising had been changed from 20 April, the original proposed date, to 23 April. Finding no-one ready to meet it, the ship waited for 24 hours, but was spotted and pursued by British patrol boats. As the *Aud* was being escorted to Queenstown (Cobh) harbour on 22 April, Captain Karl Spindler decided to scuttle the ship and its cargo, and the indispensable arms went to the bottom of the sea. The crew was rescued and interned for the duration of the war.

On Spy Wednesday, 19 April, a document called the 'Castle Document' was revealed to a meeting of Dublin Corporation. This purported to come from Dublin Castle, and contained a list of names of suspected subversives, along with plans to arrest them. It targeted all nationalist groups, not just the Irish Volunteers; people such as prominent leaders of the Gaelic League and Sinn Féin (decidedly non-violent organisations) were listed for arrest. The document was published the following day in *New Ireland*.

MacNeill and Pearse were convinced by it, and MacDiarmada swore a few hours before his execution that it was genuine, but the Castle instantly denounced it as a complete forgery. Later evidence given to the Royal Commission of Enquiry that followed the Rising seems to indicate that there had indeed been some kind of list which could have been the basis of the published one, but that it was not designed for immediate action. The original list may have been leaked from the Castle and then 'doctored' before publication. At the time, Joseph Plunkett was suspected of having either written or altered the document, with the intention of raising the public temperature, but his fiancée Grace Gifford recalled writing it down as Plunkett translated the code in which it was written.[29]

MacNeill issued a general order warning of a plot on the part of the government to disarm the Volunteers; they were to resist this by force if necessary. Meanwhile Connolly was informing his ICA officers that the Rising would be launched on Easter Sunday, and that arms were on their way from Germany. All that week, recalls Staff-Captain Seán T Ó Ceallaigh, 'Shops like Lawlors of Fownes Street which made a speciality of selling Volunteer equipment were full from morning till night with Volunteers seeking to purchase equipment of various kinds ... At no time did Clarke or MacDiarmada ... ever tell me definitely that the Rising was to take place on Easter Sunday ... I had to deduce that for myself'.[30]

On Holy Thursday, Eithne McSwiney, a Cumann na mBan courier, was sent from Cork to arrange a meeting between her brother Terry, Volunteer leader in Cork, and Clarke, MacDiarmada and Connolly. 'Terry ... feared that the dual control of the Volunteer organisation, which they knew existed in Dublin, would result in uncertainty and possibly in conflicting or even contradictory orders'. Clarke insisted that it would be impossible for McSwiney to come himself to Dublin: 'Everyone is being watched closely'. Eithne continues, 'He then began to talk, confidently and exultantly, of the victory which, he said, was assured. He was exhilarated. His whole spirit seemed to burn in his glowing eyes. He spoke with enthusiasm of help from Germany, and said that John Devoy had a document, signed by the Kaiser, recognising the Republic of Ireland.' Eithne was puzzled by this, and a little disturbed: 'I had no idea that the Volunteers were in definite contact with Germany. I told him that I thought relying on Germany was a great mistake, that every time we relied on foreign aid we were disappointed. He just pooh-poohed my fears'.[31] When she returned with Clarke's message, Terry went to Tralee, County Kerry, to discuss the situation with other commanders.

On Holy Thursday night, Bulmer Hobson learned that orders were being sent to Dublin Volunteer companies about Easter Sunday manoeuvres, without the authorisation of MacNeill. He and MacNeill immediately confronted Pearse at St Enda's, and Pearse admitted the Rising plans, telling MacNeill that the Volunteers had always been under IRB control and would now obey only Pearse himself. Hobson insisted that a Rising under these circumstances would contravene the IRB's constitution. MacNeill, returning home, issued orders cancelling any orders sent out by Pearse, and Hobson started sending these around the country.

That same day, Holy Thursday, Kathleen had gone to Limerick with despatches for the Volunteers there, and took the opportunity to bring her three sons to be left with their aunts. This would not necessarily ensure their safety, because Limerick was also expected to rise, but she wanted to be free during Easter Week to carry out any duties necessary. Tom Clarke did not say a proper goodbye to his sons; he did not want to upset them, and was afraid that the emotion would be too much for him. She carried a final note from Ned Daly to his mother. She also had a verbal message for the Limerick Volunteers, telling them that MacNeill had agreed to sign the Proclamation.

She was annoyed to find that the Limerick Commandant, Michael Colivet, wanted to hold a meeting of his officers before sending back a reply, so she had to stay overnight. She had plenty to do in Dublin, but instead found herself helping her sisters to make up First Aid outfits for Cumann na mBan. They were all wildly excited, expecting success, but she was unable to enter into their enthusiasm. Arriving back on Good Friday evening, she expressed reservations to her husband about the Limerick Volunteers and their readiness for action, much to MacDiarmada's irritation: 'You are always croaking!' She forgave him; by this stage they were all living on their nerves.[32]

That Good Friday, the Military Council had arrested Bulmer Hobson and put him under guard in a house in Cabra Park. They apparently felt that he was more likely than MacNeill to try to influence the Volunteers against a Rising, and wanted to keep him out of the way. He was distressed by this arrest, but did not show any animosity towards his captors, members of Ned Daly's First Battalion. He was released on the afternoon of Easter Monday, after the Rising had begun.

Cumann na mBan courier Kitty O'Doherty, summoned to Clarke's shop, was sent to MacNeill's office in Dawson Street to see what was happening. 'They were tearing up things and pulling out everything.' MacNeill gave her a parcel with his private papers; 'Hoey, the detective who was always haunting me, was standing at the lamp-post ... I took home his parcel'.[33] MacNeill was obviously expecting arrest. Later on Good Friday, Seán MacDiarmada informed Mac-Neill that a shipment of arms from Germany was imminent, and MacNeill agreed that this put a different complexion on things. He seems now to have agreed to sign the Proclamation, and to resign command in favour of Pearse, but it is all very unclear. His own view of a 'Rising' may have simply been armed resistance to any attempt to disarm the Volunteers, reactive rather than proactive.

On Saturday morning, Kitty O'Doherty's husband arrived home with a big case of guns from Derry. 'It was well known that the guns were coming. It was like bees around a jampot because the crowd were ardent to get the revolvers', she recalls. Leaving her children, Kitty had to spend the afternoon making trips to Lawlor's buying webbing and water bottles for Volunteers coming to her house. 'Eily O'Hanrahan told me that she had been on a message to Enniscorthy and Wexford, that she had not delivered it but had eaten it' (presumably because she was followed). Volunteers all over the city were preparing for the following day's events: Volunteer Seamus Daly recalled, 'I wasn't at all surprised to find Marlborough Street [church] filled with young men … all the one thing, going to Confession'.[34]

On Saturday afternoon, MacNeill finally learned of the arrest of Casement and the loss of the German arms, and knew the chance of success was lost. Again he confronted Pearse, to be told, 'We have used your name and influence for what they were worth, but we have done with you now. It is no use trying to stop us'. Pearse insisted that the Volunteers would no longer obey MacNeill, but MacNeill immediately went home and began to draft a countermand order for the following day. Ó Ceallaigh recalls that MacNeill asked him 'did I think it likely that the Volunteers would accept Pearse's order rather than his … I felt certain that … those who were members of the IRB or under IRB influence would accept Pearse's orders. He seemed surprised at this, greatly surprised'.[35] Liam Ó Briain quotes Desmond FitzGerald as saying that MacNeill would have had the support of a majority, four out of seven, of the Volunteer Executive for cancellation; The O'Rahilly, O'Connor, Fitzgibbon and himself.

Ó Briain argues, rather speciously, that MacNeill had

increasingly absented himself from Executive meetings, 'to slip back into the tenth century and the Book of the Dun Cow'; MacNeill was a professor of early Irish history in University College Dublin, and presumably had to give some time to the day job. If he frequently left the chairmanship to Pearse, says Ó Briain, he had surely lost the moral right to be offended 'when he suddenly came back to modern times and found that things had been done unknown to him'. But of course MacNeill, however naïve, was entitled to expect trust and fair dealing from his Executive committee, whether he was present or not.[36]

On Saturday evening, visitors arrived for the Clarkes from the north, coming for instructions and money. One of them was Denis McCullough, and when he was leaving he said to Tom Clarke, 'You carried this thing at a meeting at which I was not present. Well, let it pass now, but when this is all over, I'll have it out with you'. He clearly felt betrayed by Clarke and MacDiarmada, but would do his duty. McCullough ultimately ordered his men to stay in Belfast; once the *Aud* guns had been lost, he felt the affair was hopeless, and he could not risk their lives. He remained at his own home till he was arrested, later being imprisoned in Belfast, Dublin and Knutsford prisons.[37]

Arthur Griffith, leader of Sinn Féin, was another who felt cheated by the outbreak of the rebellion; the leadership had promised to keep him informed.[38] Pat McCartan, of the IRB

Executive, was furious that the Executive had been kept in the dark: 'The whole business was like a thunderbolt to me and I blame Tom and MacDermott entirely, and especially Tom for I trusted so much to him…'[39] However, according to his witness statement he seems to have been fairly well informed, having spent Holy Thursday night in Clarke's home, and listened to Clarke being enthusiastic about the German help they were expecting. When he sent word to ask about Casement's arrest the following day, he was told that Clarke said 'It is hopeless, but we must go on'. He may not have been informed about the changed plans.[40]

On Saturday evening, Tom and Kathleen left their home together for the last time; the Rising was to take place the following day, starting at 4pm. He was going to stay at Fleming's Hotel in Gardiner Street; he had arranged that all the leaders would stay at various safe houses that night, for fear of arrest. The couple walked to the corner of Parnell Street: 'Though both of us feared it might be our final parting, we dared not say so. We dared not indulge in goodbyes … goodbyes would break us and leave us unfit for anything'.

Later that Saturday night, 22 April, Kathleen Clarke was disturbed in the shop by Pat McCartan's sister, who had come from the north with an urgent message for Clarke. Looking for him, they called at the home of Mrs Kissane, a member of Cumann na mBan, on Hardwicke Street. There they found a meeting in progress of almost all the leadership, MacDiarmada, MacDonagh, Pearse, Plunkett, Éamonn Ceannt and others – but not Tom Clarke. The message Miss McCartan had brought was that unless there was a guarantee that the German arms had been landed, the north would not rise. MacDiarmada said, 'My God, that is the worst we heard yet'.

Kathleen asked Seán about the newspaper report that morning, some arrest on the Kerry coast, and also asked why Clarke was not at the meeting. MacDiarmada protested that they knew he needed his rest, and had not wanted to disturb him. Kathleen could see well that something terrible had happened, and insisted that Clarke should have been included, and would be very angry at this exclusion.[41] MacDonagh had found out by accident about MacNeill's countermand plan, and had called together as many of the leaders as he could to decide what to do. As they had all been dispersed to 'safe houses', rather than their own homes, this took a long time. And Tom Clarke was left out. As has been noted by Foy and Barton, 'whatever the other members' justification for ignoring him … they had diminished his authority', and Ceannt and MacDonagh were now making their voices heard more distinctly.[42]

On Easter Sunday morning, MacNeill's newspaper announcements cancelled all Volunteer 'activities' planned for that day. Clarke, having joined the Military Council meeting (now at Liberty Hall), argued vehemently for the Rising to take place as planned that afternoon; the odds were they would all be arrested that night if they did not move. However, the others outvoted him; the countermand notices would have caused confusion all over the country, and the men could never be contacted in time with a rebuttal. Instead, it was agreed to start the Rising the following day, Easter Monday, and spend the intervening hours contacting as many Volunteers as possible. Clarke was heartbroken; no-one had backed him up, not even his close friend Mac-Diarmada.

Perhaps Clarke was right, and they should have pushed ahead; the turnout on Sunday, before news of the countermand spread, was much greater than the eventual muster on Monday. Hundreds of Volunteers had turned out for manoeuvres up and down the country, only to be stood down. Conflicting messages were passed; the Military Council issued a message confirming the Sunday cancellation, and a second message ordering a start to operations at noon on Easter Monday. The confusion was intense – here was an example of how the IRB's secrecy and the Volunteers' divided leadership compounded an already complicated situation.[43] Many obviously didn't bother to turn out the following day.

Kathleen Clarke spent all Sunday afternoon at home waiting for the first shots to be fired, but could hear nothing. She could not leave the house, in case messengers arrived, so had no way of finding out what was going on. Piaras Béaslaí remembers escorting Clarke to a house on the north side that evening, and that Clarke was unexpectedly emotional, saying, 'All our elaborate plans are spoiled by this. I feel like going away to a corner to cry'.[44] Béaslaí may then have handed him over to other escorts, because Kathleen recollects seeing him arrive with Tommy O'Connor and Seán McGarry: 'Tom looked old and bent, and his walk, which was usually very quick and military, was slow.'

Clarke drank an egg flip with whiskey, although he normally did not touch liquor, but refused to eat anything. He described the events of the day to her, and accused MacNeill of treachery; he felt MacNeill should have left the decision up to the Military Council, and that his countermanding action had been dishonourable. It is hardly surprising, though, that MacNeill did not trust the Military Council; it had never trusted him, and he felt deeply betrayed.

McGarry and O'Connor were to spend the night in Clarkes' in case any attempt was made to arrest Tom. Kathleen says, 'I had a pistol and knew how to use it, and if necessary meant to take a hand … it was to be a fight to the finish'. She does not say that her brother Ned was also in the house – he was living with the Clarkes – but other sources confirm that he was. There was no raid that night, but an old man named Ryan who had heard of the Rising plans came in and shouted at Tom, 'asking was he mad, what was going to happen to his wife and family, hadn't he suffered enough for Ireland?' Eventually he left, still protesting, and Tom and

Kathleen went to bed. 'I slept in my husband's arms for the last time that night, and slept soundly.'[45]

Meanwhile, the Dublin Castle administration seems to have woken up at last. On Easter Sunday, Lord Wimborne wrote to Birrell, who was in London, telling him about Casement's arrest and the loss of the German arms. Nathan proposed that raids should take place on Liberty Hall and other places where arms were known to be stored, and that arrests should also take place, but it was agreed to wait for Birrell's consent before doing anything. They would be too late.

Historian Maureen Wall has written that the excessive secrecy of the Military Council would probably have worked against success, even if all the plans had worked out. There was no proper chain of command; some were in the know, some were not. 'Absolute secrecy maintained by a tiny group of men, who were relying on the unquestioning obedience of the members of a nationwide revolutionary organization, was bound to defeat their object of bringing about a revolution, except in Dublin where these men were, in fact, in a position to control events'. She argues that it was useless to put IRB men in key positions if they did not even know of the existence of the Military Council, or of the deep divisions in the Volunteer leadership.[46] This lack of communication was of major importance in the wake of the later conflicting orders and countermands from Pearse and MacNeill; the Limerick Volunteers, for example, decided that they would only rise on orders from MacNeill, not from Pearse. They were not in the IRB 'know', and Limerick did not rise.

On Easter Monday morning, the Military Council assembled in Liberty Hall. At about 11.50, the Irish Citizen Army (or as many as had turned out), accompanied by the Military Council and a number of Volunteers and Cumann na mBan members, marched away from Liberty Hall, down Abbey Street and into Sackville (now O'Connell) Street. The parade included two wagons loaded with weaponry. Tom Clarke and Seán MacDiarmada travelled in a cab so as not to slow down the march, although Joseph Plunkett, in the last stages of TB, insisted on walking. There were about 150 men and women in all, later called the Headquarters Battalion. Watching citizens and policemen were mildly interested; they had seen such marches often before. Clarke had been observed in Liberty Hall as 'very happy' by Garry Holohan, who helped him into his coat because of the injured right arm;[47] Patrick O'Daly also says he helped Tom into his equipment, so he was well looked after.[48] He did not wear a uniform, but he carried a revolver and a bandolier.

When the parade arrived in Sackville Street, opposite the Imperial Hotel, James Connolly ordered it to wheel left and charge the GPO. The GPO was cleared of disbelieving customers and staff, sometimes forcibly. Any British mili-

tary found were taken into custody, including three officers (Clarke later arranged for letters to be brought to their
wives). As the most prominent building taken over by the
revolutionaries, the GPO became the place to go for dozens
of Volunteers, ICA and Cumann na mBan who could not
find their own units, or whose units had failed to muster.
There was no roll-call taken during that hectic week, and the
numbers in the GPO and the surrounding area will never be
fully established, but Diarmuid Lynch finally estimated it to
be just over four hundred people by the end of the week. As
well as the GPO, other buildings were taken over in Sackville
Street, and eventually the whole street from Henry Street
to the river was occupied, as well as some of the buildings
facing the river.

Tom Clarke gave the Proclamation to Patrick Pearse, and
sent him out to the front of the GPO to read it to the passing crowds. This was met with a mixture of bafflement and
derision, and few people paused to listen. They were more
impressed when two flags were raised over the GPO, an Irish
tricolour and a green flag with a golden harp painted on it.
The Irish Citizen Army flag, the 'starry plough', was raised
over the Imperial Hotel, owned by one of Connolly's toughest employer adversaries, William Martin Murphy. Copies of
the Proclamation were pasted up around the streets.

Meanwhile the other Battalion headquarters were being
established: Ned Daly's First Battalion in the Four Courts,

MacDonagh's Second Battalion at Jacob's Factory, Éamon de Valera's Third Battalion at Boland's Bakery, Ceannt's Fourth Battalion in the South Dublin Union, and Thomas Ashe's Fifth Battalion in County Dublin, outside the city. The main ICA force, under Michael Mallin, took over the Stephen's Green area.

The news broke like a thunderbolt in the Viceregal Lodge, in Phoenix Park, where Lord Lieutenant Wimborne was feeling confident that the cancellation of manoeuvres had averted disaster. At 12.30, a telephone message from the police announced that the Castle had been attacked, the GPO seized, Stephen's Green occupied, the Ashtown railway bridge destroyed, and that the insurgents were marching on the Viceregal Lodge. Lord Wimborne wrote a rapid dispatch to Chief Secretary Birrell, saying 'the worst has happened just when we thought it averted. The Post Office is seized – Nathan still besieged in the Castle, but I hope he will soon be out. Almost all wires cut. Bridges blown up. Everybody away on holiday'.[49] To celebrate the Easter holiday, almost all the British officers in Dublin had set off to the Fairyhouse races in County Meath, and the GOC Irish Command, Major-General Friend, had gone to London for the weekend.

Five signatories of the Proclamation remained in the GPO during Easter Week – Clarke, Pearse, MacDiarmada, Plunkett and Connolly. Ceannt and MacDonagh had their own commands. Connolly, as commander of the Dublin area, spent much of his time sending orders and messages around the other areas. He would dictate these messages to his secretary, Winifred Carney, who had accompanied him with her typewriter. He frequently went the rounds of the Sackville Street barricades to check how things were going, his calm demeanour heartening nervous Volunteers, but was badly injured later in the week on one of these sorties, when a ricocheting bullet fractured his ankle bone.

The first skirmish was unintentionally provoked by a group of British lancers who came trotting down Sackville Street, unaware of what was happening. They were greeted by a volley of shots, which brought down both horses and riders, killing three men. At least one horse was killed also, and its putrefying corpse figures largely in reminiscences, as the smell became intolerable over the next few days.

Tom Clarke spent the whole of Easter Week in the GPO, giving a hand wherever required. He was an inspiration to the fighting young people around him, an iconic figure who had suffered many years in prison for Ireland's sake. Indeed, they took very good care of him, making sure he had somewhere comfortable to sleep and enough to eat, although he protested he did not need or want any special treatment. He took the time to speak to a number of them privately, hoping that they would survive to bring out his message, of a hoped-for Republic and a new Ireland.

Clarke and MacDiarmada were essentially non–combatants, but their authority was unquestioned. Those Volunteers who were not IRB members would not necessarily have recognised them, but could see the respect given to them by Pearse, Plunkett and Connolly. Neither Clarke nor Mac-Diarmada had any formal military rank but they now intervened to issue promotions, give instructions on the movement of munitions and prisoners, and command Volunteer parties who fought the fires that swept the GPO on Friday.'[50] Crisis meetings were held from time to time, in response to British troop movements and shelling. Clarke also kept an eye on morale; he would go around giving out cigarettes and tobacco (he may have brought supplies from the shop). William Daly recalls how he gave them all bars of chocolate, and had a chat with each of them.[51]

However, Clarke was adamant about the use of alcohol; when a small bar was discovered in the GPO, he insisted that all the beer and stout should be poured away, leaving only the soft drinks.[52] One Volunteer, Joe Gahan, objected to this, and insisted on having a surreptitious glass of beer in the corner, keeping an eye out for Clarke's return. Clarke did come back to check his orders had been carried out; he did not want anyone to be tempted to drink. He spent the early afternoon of Monday reading through the reports found in the RIC pigeonholes relating to the Volunteers.[53]

One Volunteer later wrote a stirring account of the scene: 'In the building itself all the lower storey windows have been barricaded with bags of mail, boxes of sand, ironwork, chairs, tables etc. Through roughly-formed loopholes one catches sight of glistening, exultant faces, shining gun barrels and well-stocked bandoliers. From all sides resounds the nerve-shattering jar of breaking glass, and occasionally the hoarse orders of unseen officers ... Armourers have collected all the loose and spare ammunition, rifles, revolvers, pikes etc, into one central depot. Another room has been set apart for hand and fuse grenades'.[54]

The GPO was built around a large open square, and most of the central hall was now screened off as a hospital. 'A kit-store had been opened in another portion, and here boots, handkerchiefs, trousers, shirts, overcoats, combs and boot-laces were to be obtained, while the sorting-tables were in general use as sleeping-bunks ... In a secluded corner a priest sat hearing confessions...' Arranged around the central hall were the main buildings, and all the windows looking onto the streets were manned by riflemen. 'Behind the riflemen were squads labouring feverishly, building new defences and consolidating old ones.'[55]

Kathleen Clarke received messages regularly from the GPO until mid-week, when the surrounding battles made streets impassable. On Easter Monday, her husband had sent her a copy of the Proclamation by special messenger; she later presented this to the Kilmainham Gaol Museum. She was responsible for doling out money for incidental expenses, sending it in by the couriers, and the NLI Clarke Papers contain a hastily written list of the money paid out that week, amounting to over £2,000.[56] Kathleen remembers that Sorcha MacMahon, a Cumann na mBan courier, told her, 'Mr Pearse would make you laugh; he was going around the GPO like one in a dream, getting in the way of those trying to get things in order, and Mr Clarke said, "For God's sake will someone get that man an office and a desk, with paper and pens, and set him down to write"'.[57]

During that week, Pearse produced a paper called *Irish War News*. He also periodically made speeches to his forces in the GPO, encouraging them with news of how the others in Dublin were doing, and improvising positive news about other areas. Townshend remarks that it really didn't matter whether he or his listeners really believed all this; 'The power of the belief clearly overwhelmed doubt'.[58] Meanwhile, in Abbey Street, a group of Volunteers had taken over a telegraph office, and broadcast the news of the rising to the world.

Plunkett, who had devised the war plan, began to make notes about the other HQ sites, as messengers arrived; he may have been trying to assess how much had gone according to plan, what with all the orders and countermands. One account describes him moving among the men with 'gentle urgings and praise'. Tom Clarke was equally excited: Desmond FitzGerald recalls him being elated that Ireland had indeed risen, even if it was only a few who had done so. He was bitterly angry about the countermanding order. FitzGerald wondered what the prospects were, but did not get a clear answer; Clarke reiterated that it would have been a great fight if there had been no countermand but, FitzGerald says, 'he did not by any means say that even in that case it would have been a victorious fight, or even a fight whose outcome could conceivably have been in our favour'.[59]

The leaders rested in turn behind the great central counter on the ground floor, first on mattresses and later on beds brought in for them. Sleep was only possible in short spells, with the noise and the heat, and in fact the Red Cross members of the Volunteers gave some of the leaders sleeping draughts, probably opium. 'Early in the week the leaders could be seen seated together in quiet moments on boxes and barrels, chatting in low tones; calm, pale, tired, sometimes laughing as when Connolly announced that the Citizen Army had captured King George and Kitchener in the Henry Street Waxworks.'[60]

Frank O'Connor depicts Clarke as harassed and excited, 'blaming everyone for the mistakes which had been made', but this is not how he was seen by others.[61] Charles MacAuley, a surgeon called to the GPO, was impressed by the sight of Tom Clarke, sitting 'with a bandolier across his shoulders and a rifle between his knees … He was silent and had a look of grim determination on his face. It was as if he thought his day had come. He never spoke'. Seán McGarry also commented on Clarke's cool demeanour:'His normal air of business seemed to have been accentuated and he gave his orders decisively and as calmly as if he were in his own shop'.[62]

Leslie Price (later Bean de Barra) and Bríd Dixon, two Cumann na mBan members, headed for the GPO when they heard it was occupied. Clarke told them they would be used as couriers, but later sent Leslie over to the Hibernian Bank at the corner of Abbey Street to take charge of the Cumann na mBan there. They had to evacuate that building on the Wednesday, and returned to the GPO. Here Leslie continued to act as a courier to Ned Daly in the Four Courts, travelling through cavities in the walls and eerily quiet streets each night, when all was dark. One night she and Bríd came back from one of these journeys to find that the GPO restaurant was open only for officers. They were starving, so MacDiarmada and Clarke agreed to make them officers for the night: Leslie remarks, 'We were made officers on the battlefield I always said afterwards'.[63]

The leaders were distressed to see the outbreak of looting in the streets, before the fusillade of bullets and the spreading flames made it too dangerous for civilians to venture out. The poorer inhabitants of Dublin found the temptations of streets without any visible law too much for them, and an orgy of theft began. Neighbours invited one another to 'hoolies' (parties) to eat the stolen food and drink; some were wheeling a piano up North Great George's Street.[64] Manfield's boot shop, at the corner of Abbey Street, was looted, and streams of people walked past with piles of boots and shoes. Volunteers fired in the air to discourage them, but without success: 'Clery's store, a large one, was like an ant heap. Men, women and children swarmed about, carrying off furniture, silks, satins; pushing baby carriages filled with sheets, stockings, garters, curtains'.[65]

Luke Kennedy, an engineer, pointed out to Tom Clarke early in the week that the water might be cut off – that if he was among the forces attacking the GPO, he would have all the utilities cut off, to force them out. Pearse, at first doubtful, finally agreed that provision should be made, and a group went up to the Dairy Engineering Company in Bachelors' Walk, collected milk churns, and kept them filled with water for the week.

Patrick Rankin from Dundalk, whom Clarke had known previously, managed to make his way to the GPO on Tuesday. He remembers that Clarke 'looked about thirty years younger and seemed so happy you would imagine you were talking to him in his old shop in Parnell Street.' Clarke was pleased to see Rankin, but regretted that there were not more fighters from the north.[66]

As shells began to hit Sackville Street on Wednesday from the gunship *Helga*, and the flames from burning buildings moved closer to the GPO, Plunkett said excitedly, 'It's the first time this has happened since Moscow! The first time a capital city has burned since 1812!'[67] British troops had been hastily requisitioned from England, and had landed in Dublin on Tuesday night. Some were under the impression that they were in France, which they had been training for.

Clarke was delighted to welcome from Limerick Éamonn de hÓir, a medical student who was MacDiarmada's aide-de-camp. He had gone home for Easter, as many other students had done – MacDiarmada had given them permission to do so – and had travelled back with Laura and Nora Daly, nieces of John. Clarke must have been glad to get news of Limerick, although it was not encouraging. The two girls, experienced Cumann na mBan couriers, were given messages to bring to Cork and Limerick, urging the Volunteers there to come out and distract British forces in that part of the country.

Éamonn then went to his digs in Gardiner Street to get his rifle, talking his way through various British barricades, but found that other friends had taken it for safety, and given it to a Volunteer who then did not turn out. Frustrated, he made his way back to the GPO, through the British checkpoints and the whistling bullets, and was finally let in through the back gate. 'I … fell into the arms of the sentry. The next I can remember is the exclamation from Tom Clarke, just passing as I steadied myself, "Éamonn, so you got back".' He and Clarke discussed the situation. De hÓir still thought it would be possible to fight their way out; if not, the pincers would soon close. He helped Clarke with the work of finding stores and moving material from one floor to another.[68]

Members of the general public were still wandering around, seemingly oblivious to the danger in the streets. Later that day, though, things began to hot up; a machine gun placed on the Brunswick Fire Station began to pepper the GPO, sounding like a burst of hail. It was soon silenced by the GPO snipers.

On Thursday morning, Clarke showed Desmond FitzGerald a small concrete room in a back yard, and said that he was now promoted (the rank was not specified), and that when the time came he was to gather all the girls in there and defend them to the last. 'It means', Clarke said, 'that if you are not killed beforehand, you will be taken by the enemy and probably executed.' Understandably shaken by this prospect, FitzGerald found himself focusing on whether he should be shot or hanged. Clarke said that he would probably be shot, but added, 'they may keep to the hanging. The English love hanging.' FitzGerald accepted his new responsibility, 'though I was far from feeling happy about it'.[69]

That Thursday the garrison was ordered to prepare for a siege, and moved many sacks of coal from the Post Office yard to serve as barricades, working from 5am to midday. However, as shells continued to fall and the risk of fire increased, they were ordered to bring all the coal back out to the yard.[70] Pearse made a stirring speech in which he outlined the achievements of the various Battalions, announced that a large band of Volunteers was coming from Dundalk, and, most importantly, insisted that since they had now held out for three days as a republic, they would be entitled under international law to send a delegation to any post-war peace talks. This caused a deafening cheer.

Later on Thursday, Tom Clarke sent Leslie Price to bring back a priest from Marlborough Street church. She was terrified, but ashamed to show fear in front of him ('he had sort of steely eyes'), and managed to reach Marlborough Street by keeping close to the walls and crossing Sackville Street by the Parnell Monument. The priest she spoke to said, 'Do you realise that you're working in there with a group of communists, that you have James Connolly and all the socialists in there? ... I'm certain no man or woman in the GPO wants a priest.' She insisted that he come with her, however, and he finally did, staying for some time in the GPO; in fact, Tom Clarke insisted that he was not to be let out.[71]

Le Roux's account says that this priest was objectionable to the garrison, being opposed to the revolutionaries, and was replaced by Father John Flanagan, to whom Pearse sent a personal request.[72] However, most sources agree that the priest brought back by Leslie Price was actually Father Flanagan (or O'Flanagan), who stayed till the end, collecting letters and wills from many of the men, hearing confessions and giving the last rites. Foy and Barton state that Father

Flanagan was summoned by Pearse from the pro-Cathedral, on Easter Monday night.[73]

Min Ryan recounts a conversation with Tom Clarke on Thursday night. She describes him as beaming every time a shell burst: 'I have never seen him look happier – he was like a bride at a wedding'.[74] He went over the reasons for the Rising – the need to win Ireland a place at the peace conference, the need to rouse the national spirit, and the need to give the Volunteers an aim – and said that although the leaders would die, those that escaped would carry on the fight. He seems to have had much the same conversation with Min's brother James, and with several other young people, obviously with the intention of encouraging as many survivors as possible to speak for the Rising after its leaders were dead.[75] James Ryan adds that Clarke gave the reasons for rising when they did, but was also careful to list the arguments that had been made against the timing of the Rising.[76]

The fires continued. 'Some oil works near Abbey Street is singed by the conflagration, and immediately a solid sheet of blinding, death-white flame rushes hundreds of feet into the air with a thunderous explosion that shakes the walls. It is followed by a heavy bombardment as hundreds of drums of oil explode. The intense light compels one to close the eyes. Even here [the GPO] the heat is so terrible that it strikes one like a solid thing as blasts of scorching air come in through the glassless windows. Millions of sparks are floating in impenetrable masses for hundreds of yards around O'Connell Street, and as a precaution we are ordered to drench the barricades with water again.'[77]

'Songs were sung through the night', remembers Aoife de Burca, such as 'A Nation Once Again', and they nearly brought down the roof.[78] The Rosary was also recited frequently by Cumann na mBan; almost all the Volunteers carried rosary beads around their necks.

By Friday, it was clear that the GPO would have to be abandoned. The flames were getting closer, and the ammunition in the basement was at risk of explosion. Fires had broken out in the roof and other areas, and the water hoses had stopped working. Clarke said, 'Things are looking serious now; we are surrounded'.[79] The leaders had probably agreed by this time that they would try to escape, rather than burn with the building.

That evening, Tom Clarke moved the prisoners to the cellar, telling them that it was the only place of safety, and that the Volunteers were going to make a last stand. He assured them that if the building was abandoned, the prisoners would come with them. He then had a meal with Seán MacDiarmada, Diarmuid Lynch and Seán McGarry; they joked that they might go to hell for eating meat on a Friday, and Clarke then opened a tin of pears with a bayonet.[80] People had spent the week complaining about the food rationing, because Desmond FitzGerald, in charge of it, was extremely stingy with the portions. However, he was justified; by the end, the building contained far more people than had been originally planned, and he needed to keep enough supplies for ten days.

Word reached them that the GPO itself was on fire. They went down and helped to carry bombs from a danger point to one less dangerous. De hÓir mentions that his hat caught fire and was destroyed, but he was not hurt. However, the end had obviously been reached, and a decision was made to abandon the stricken building.

Chapter Seven

Endgame and After

Stunned by the noise of the guns and the flames, choking in the dense smoke of the burning building, Tom Clarke joined the other exhausted members of the GPO garrison who gathered on Friday night at a side door into Henry Street. The prisoners had been set free to take their chances, and the wounded were being escorted out on the other side of the building. The leaders' plan seems to have been to try and reach Williams and Woods, a jam factory on Parnell Street. There they could make a last stand, or perhaps even escape to the mountains.

The O'Rahilly, Arms Director of the Volunteers, had initially wanted the Rising postponed, but when it started he joined the garrison in the GPO. Now he gathered a small group of Volunteers to strike against the British barricade at the junction of Henry Street and Mary Street, hoping to break through to Williams and Woods, or at least to create a diversion to enable others to escape. Most of those who followed him up Henry Street died; The O'Rahilly himself was wounded, managed to reach Sackville Lane, and died there some hours later. Others thought better of this doomed sortie, and turned back to the GPO.[1]

Patrick Pearse stood by the small side door, and each time he dropped his sword, as the firing lessened briefly, a group of Volunteers would race across the street towards Henry Place. In the end, as the flames pressed closer, discipline was forgotten; those remaining burst out and ran pell-mell for the shelter of the lanes. No-one is quite sure who was the last to leave the GPO; Kathleen Clarke says Clarke told her that he was last, having checked that it was finally empty, but others place Pearse as the last to leave. It seems that Harry Boland and Diarmuid Lynch were actually the last, as they had been checking the ammunition in the basement and had missed the order to evacuate. Astonished to find the hall deserted when they came up the stairs, they hurried after the others.[2] Leslie Price said the last person she saw coming out of the GPO was Tom Clarke. He shook her hand and said, 'If you see my wife' –Stopping for a moment, he continued, 'Tell her the men were wonderful to the…' He could not continue, but she knew he meant 'end'; she saw that he was very pent up.[3]

Desmond FitzGerald, in charge of supplies, had arranged for food to be carried out by the retreating garrison, and lamented that a large amount had to be left behind. 'I had to laugh as I thought of the rigour with which I had refused more than a bare minimum to the men through the week, and made them detest me, only to leave the most of it here to be burnt'.[4] Having sorted out the food, he helped to evacuate the eighteen wounded under a white flag, through nearby houses, into Prince's Street and from there into Abbey Street. They were then taken to hospital. Their escort, including Willie Pearse, arrived back just in time to join the retreat.

The garrison survivors worked their way along the back lanes, under continuous fire from British barricades, and from snipers on top of the Rotunda Hospital to the north of them and Amiens Street station to the east. In Henry Place, James Connolly was laid on the ground on a stretcher, as his ankle had been shattered by a bullet on Thursday. Tom Clarke tried to shoot the lock off a door, without success – probably the first time he had used his firearm during the week. A motor van was dragged from O'Brien's Mineral Water Works (the building is still extant) and placed across Moore Lane as a partial protection against the snipers.

Volunteers Henry Coyle and Michael Mulvihill died on that panic-stricken journey, as did two civilians – a Volunteer shot the lock on the door of her home in Henry Place, seeking shelter, and Brigid McKane, aged 15, died when the bullet went through her father's shoulder and hit her. William Mullen, aged nine, was also shot, but the circumstances of his death are unknown. Some men climbed up to the roofs, hoping to escape that way, but the flames drove them back to the ground.

It was decided to gain entry into the houses in Moore Street, and try to get from there to Williams and Woods. Connolly was being carried along in a sheet. His command responsibilities were handed over to the twenty-one-year-old Seán McLoughlin, a Fianna member who had already displayed courage and military ability as a courier; Seán MacDiarmada recommended him, and Connolly agreed. Only three women were still with them: Connolly's secretary, Winifred Carney, and the nurses Elizabeth O'Farrell and Julia Grenan.

Breaking through a door in the first house in the Moore Street terrace, No 10, Cogan's shop, the Volunteers began to move through the 18th-century terrace, tunnelling through the thin walls. The leaders remained in Cogan's while this took place, and Charles Saurin describes Tom Clarke sitting in a corner with his hands around his knees. 'A Volunteer beside him was irritably taxing him with taking his place [his seat] … I thought this was going too far and leaned across and told him who he was attacking…' Leo Henderson then came in and told Clarke that he had a bed for him: 'Tom Clarke got up and with difficulty made his way over the men stretched out on the floor'.[5]

Apart from Cogan's, where the terrified family had taken shelter in the basement, the houses were nearly all deserted.

'What a queer life!' remembered Fergus Burke, 'Creeping through holes into bedrooms, then downstairs and through another opening into sitting rooms, through shops, and finally to our resting place for the night'.[6] By the following day, the tunnelling had reached the far corner house of the terrace, and the 300-odd men and three women settled in for a siege. The leaders were urged to stay in Nos. 15 and 16, the central houses of the terrace, as being probably the safest.

They were cut off from any information, but they all knew from the flames and the bombardment that they must be surrounded, and that their options were growing more limited by the hour. As the sun set and the firing died down, a massive explosion was heard; the flames had reached the ammunition stored in the basement of the GPO. According to Kathleen, during the night Clarke wrote on a wall, 'Fifth Day, Irish Republic'. In the same house he wrote in pencil on a door jamb. She added, 'The piece of the wall and doorway were procured for me by Batt O'Connor and I think Seán T Ó Ceallaigh.'[7] The piece of wall is now in the National Museum of Ireland.

Seventeen Volunteers had been wounded in the retreat, and the nurses did their best to help them; they were brought to a hayshed in one of the back yards. The terrace remained under fire; four houses began to burn, and a shell flattened one house which they had left behind. Some of the Volunteers spent hours on Saturday morning trying to control the

flames with a few empty biscuit tins and a small water tap.
De hÓir recalls, 'Having no food we found a box of raisins
not too clean and together with water we made a meal of
them that almost poisoned us'.[8]

Again the regular prayers began, something which seemed to
irritate one ill-humoured young Volunteer, Michael Collins: Joe
Good recalled, 'I was resting on the stairs at one point with
my head in my hands and Michael said angrily to me, "Are
you ... ing praying too?"[9]

James Connolly had been brought to a first-floor room
in No. 16, and the leaders gathered around his bed for their
conferences. McLoughlin, from his travels as a courier during
the week, had the clearest view of how trapped they were,
and of the positions of the British barricades. He proposed
to lead a sortie to rush the barricade at the end of Moore
Street, while throwing a bomb. This would enable everyone
else to come out of Moore Street, run to Little Denmark
Street, and make their way to Capel Street, from where they
might be able to reach Ned Daly's command in the Four
Courts. Since this would have to be a very fast run to have
any chance at all, the wounded would have to be left behind,
apart from Connolly.

Pearse was unconvinced by the plan, fearing it would
mean more innocent civilian deaths. McLoughlin replied, 'I
am sorry, I cannot help that. This is a military operation and
I can only make it successful if I don't think about these

things'. Connolly also was distressed; he did not want to be the only wounded man saved. It was probably when considering this move that both Pearse and Connolly decided they had come far enough; Pearse had already been deeply upset by witnessing civilians being shot in Moore Street, even though they had carried white flags.

McLoughlin gathered a group together, later referring to them as his 'Death or Glory Squad'.[10] Charles Saurin mordantly described the plan: 'Apparently the seven of us … were to jump out through the open doorway down onto the lane below, fire a volley and charge the barricade. This was supposed to be a diversion while the main body … broke out into Moore Street and stormed a big barricade at the top of the street, and no doubt carried all before it in the direction of Williams and Woods while seven corpses lay in Moore Lane…'.[11] McLoughlin brought his men to No. 25 Moore Street, at the end of the terrace, and opened the door to Sackville Lane (now O'Rahilly Parade). Here they found the bodies of The O'Rahilly, Francis Macken and Charles Carrigan, and said a prayer for them. Before they could go further, McLoughlin was called back to Connolly's room, and a final Council of War was held.

By a majority vote, it was agreed to surrender; in this way the leaders hoped to save the lives of most of their followers. Tom Clarke alone stood against the decision, as he had against the decision to delay the start of the Rising. He had been through too much to see this fight end in defeat, and felt tempted to shoot himself and save the British the trouble. However, he changed his mind and decided to leave it to his enemy to kill him.[12] He also wished to keep the executive looking united, and not give anyone a chance to say that there had been a split among the leaders.[13] Connolly was insistent that he would not leave his brave ICA men to burn to death. 'MacDiarmada came to Elizabeth O'Farrell and asked her to make a white flag. Tom Clarke was standing by the window. He broke down and Winifred Carney went to him, only to burst into tears herself. They held each other for a few moments.'[14] McLoughlin took the news badly, but Clarke patted him on the back and said 'Don't take it like that, Seán; there are bigger things involved, you did your best'.[15]

The word of surrender was passed through the houses, and many of the men were angered and upset by it. The 'Kimmage Garrison' in particular, consisting mainly of British Volunteers who had trained at Joseph Plunkett's home, were particularly reluctant to surrender, as they feared being shot as deserters. Clarke, Plunkett and Collins took turns trying to persuade them, as they gathered in the back yard of No. 21, but it was Seán MacDiarmada in the end who made them listen. He assured them that they would merely be imprisoned, and would live to fight another day.

It was agreed to send one of the women out with a white

flag – a dangerous mission, considering the number of people already shot while under this fragile protection. At about 12.45am, Elizabeth O'Farrell, who had bravely volunteered for the hazardous journey, came out the door of No. 15 Moore Street, and walked slowly up the street. Her message was that Pearse wanted to discuss surrender terms. She was sent from Moore Street to Parnell Street, where the Red Cross insignia were taken from her uniform, and was brought to General Lowe, who was sitting in Tom Clarke's shop there. He listened to her, then had her driven back to Moore Street with the message that unconditional surrender was necessary, within half an hour.

She was sent out for a second time, with a note requesting other terms, but Lowe would not hear of anything but a complete surrender, and threatened to start firing again. Accepting the inevitable, Pearse went out with Nurse O'Farrell, surrendered his arms at the barricade, and signed a formal document of surrender. He was driven off to the military HQ at Parkgate Barracks, as Nurse O'Farrell prepared to bring the news of surrender to the other Commandants.[16] Meanwhile Joseph Plunkett came out of No. 16 and stood with his back to the soldiers at the Moore Street barricade and the wounded were brought out and laid on the street. Under Plunkett's orders, the rest of the survivors began to move down Moore Street. 'Filing up and forming ranks, with sloped arms, the first group marched off picking up any stragglers on the way. Next, Willie Pearse headed the main body waving his white flag. Close behind him walked Tom Clarke and towards the rear walked Seán MacDiarmada and Joseph Plunkett, supported by Julia Grenan and Winifred Carney'.[17] They marched through Henry Place and Henry Street, to O'Connell Street.[18]

They were lined up in O'Connell Street, where they awaited the arrival of other surrendered garrisons. Last to arrive was the First Battalion, marching from the Four Courts under the leadership of their Commandant, Ned Daly, who had fought a much-admired campaign throughout the week. All weapons were left at the Parnell Monument, and at least one British officer whispered to the prisoners to drop anything incriminating on the ground, so it could not be linked to them. The surrendered rebels were then herded into the front garden of the Rotunda Maternity Hospital, at the corner of Parnell Square.

That was a long, cold, miserable night. They were all hungry and thirsty, and had to relieve themselves where they sat; even the women were not exempt. Captain Lea Wilson, the most aggressive officer, walked up and down 'yelling that no-one must stand up, that no-one must lie down, and as for the needs of nature, anyone who chooses the Rotunda Gardens for a bedroom can use it as a lavatory as well, and ... ing well lie in both'.[19] There were over 400 prisoners, in a space fit for about 150. When members of the DMP arrived, they began to search for known characters; the G–Men seemed to take particular pleasure in their work.

Plunkett had asked McLoughlin to assure the men that they would be treated as prisoners-of-war when they surrendered. However, one officer berated another for talking to 'a lot of bloody rebels'. 'A hum went down the ranks as we realised the category in which we were being put and that perhaps there was not going to be so much of the prisoner of war business for us', says Saurin.[20]

Several of the leaders were harassed by British officers; Seán MacDiarmada was jeered at for his bad leg, and Plunkett was kicked. Tom Clarke was singled out by Lea Wilson, who took him off for an interrogation, shouting: 'This old bastard has been at it before. He has a shop across the street there. He's an old Fenian'. 'Tom's arm … had stiffened and in order to get his coat off …Wilson tore that arm open again'.[21] He was searched thoroughly, and it has been said that he was stripped naked in front of the windows of the nurses' home. This cannot be verified, and Louis Le Roux does not mention it in a biography which lost no chance to emphasise Clarke's sufferings for his country. However, this may have had more to do with the puritanism of 1930s Ireland, when the words 'naked' or 'stripped' would not have been printed; or perhaps Kathleen Clarke did not want this shameful episode recalled.[22]

Clarke was questioned for about an hour before being

returned to the garden, and said that the whole record of his life had been read out to him. 'Everything, they have everything', he said.[23] Brian O'Higgins remembers him as coming back cool and scornful: 'They hadn't overawed *him* at all events'.[24]

Jim Ryan woke towards morning and found his head was resting on Tom Clarke's shoulder. Clarke asked if he was awake, then said, 'I was waiting for an opportunity to turn'. 'I shall always remember this consideration for a tired young man who indeed might easily have been disturbed without suffering any loss of sleep'.[25]

The following morning, they were allowed to stand up; 'nurses who crowded at the hospital windows saw a cloud of urine steaming up from the grass'.[26] They were marched off to Richmond Barracks, Inchicore, two miles away. Passing through the city centre, they were all astonished at the devastation revealed. Some civilians, watching this stoic parade, expressed sympathy and support, but in general the public attitude was hostile, particularly that of the 'separation women', whose husbands were fighting in France. Easter Week had seen the first anniversary of the second Battle of Ypres, in which the Dublin Fusiliers had taken enormous casualties. An old woman standing near the GPO shouted, 'Look at what was trying to keep out the Government. You might as well try and keep out the ocean with a fork!'[27]

Despite the jeering and abuse, Tom Clarke marched

proudly the whole way. William Whelan, a young Volunteer, recalled that Clarke was just in front of him when they reached the barracks: 'He gave me a large sum of money. "Bill, you take this, I won't need it any more"… it could have been about £50. Clarke knew he was finished then'.[28]

When they arrived in the barracks, they were kept standing there for some time. 'The men, some of whom had been without water for nearly twenty-four hours and who had not been allowed to a lavatory of any kind during that time were fainting from sickness and pain in the yard', said Éamonn de hÓir.[29] He also saw more than one Volunteer give away his watch or other valuable for a mouthful of water. Finally they were put in the gymnasium. Here a group of G-men arrived again, and singled out those they wanted, including Ned Daly.

Piaras Béaslaí found Clarke convinced that the Rising would have a very good effect on the morale of the country.[30] 'He spoke cheerfully, confidently. "This insurrection, though it has failed, will have a wonderful effect on the country", he said. "We will die, but it will be a different Ireland after us".' Mac Diarmada agreed with him: 'There will be executions; I suppose I will be shot; but the executions will create a reaction in the country which will wipe out the slavish pro-English spirit'.[31]

Liam Ó Briain speaks of Tom Clarke 'sitting there just as we had seen him twenty times in his shop in Parnell Street, with the same clothes, the same look, quite silent, with the suspicion of a smile. Tom was very satisfied with himself and the situation … Seán [Mac Diarmada] fell asleep with his head on Tom's chest … Seán would start a little and we would hear a mutter from him saying "The fire! The fire! Get the men out!" Then you would hear Tom's quiet voice saying gently: "Quiet, Seán, we're in the barracks now. We're prisoners now, Seán"'.[32]

Joseph Gleeson describes the scene among the prisoners: 'they prayed, told stories, composed poetry, sang songs, and debated the merits of the Rising, with themselves and their guards. Despite the failure of the insurrection and the hostile public response, most of the leaders appeared confident of vindication. Tom Clarke spoke of "a minimum loss, which will result in a maximum gain"'.[33]

Éamonn de hÓir tried to pray: 'I realised how futile it was to wait for the last moment to say your prayers. If you hadn't them said before that you would never say them then'.[34]

Once the leaders had been identified and removed, the rest of the men were pushed into cells, fifty in each, and given dog biscuits and tins of bully beef. De hÓir says, 'When finally we were allowed to "relieve" ourselves … we were given a large dust-bin to use. When we were finished the bin was removed and as far as I could see, the same bin was brought back full of water. We were so mad with thirst by this time that we were not particular what was last in the bin so long as it contained water ... I could have killed anyone for a drink by this time'.[35]

Around two hundred and sixty volunteers were subsequently marched to Kilmainham Gaol, where they were kept for a week before being taken to the docks. Here they boarded a cattle boat taking them to internment in Britain. Their guards tried to frighten them by threatening that the boat would be sunk as soon as it was out to sea, but indeed the journey was so rough that many of them wished to die before it was over.

There were about eighty women prisoners, some of whom had had to insist on being arrested, as the British authorities were very unwilling to take them. They were kept for eleven days in Kilmainham Gaol, in very poor conditions. All but a dozen were then released, and ultimately only five women were sent to Britain for internment. They had had to struggle in the first place to be considered as equal combatants with the men – even many of the Volunteers queried their commitment – and now they found themselves dismissed by General Maxwell, now in charge, as 'silly little girls'.

Tom Clarke was one leader who took them seriously. Leslie Price recalled: 'I would be sent to his shop in Parnell Street with messages or despatches and he'd always bring you in and talk to you as if you were an adult and he trusted us so much that we couldn't but react to that trust by giving him trust and faithfulness afterwards'.[36] Another Cumann na mBan member said, 'He was always keen to give women a proper place in every organisation',[37] and of course his wife was very certain of his commitment to women's equality: 'He had a high opinion of women as companions and fellow-workers'.[38]

All that week, the courts martial of the leaders of the Easter Rising took place. Some of the choices made by the authorities seem odd; Willie Pearse, for instance, was probably 'tapped' simply because he was the brother of Patrick. But there was never any doubt about Tom Clarke's role, and his status as a leader. His reputation was well known, as a dynamiter and a convict. Indeed, if anyone had pleaded on his behalf for leniency on account of his age or his young family, he would undoubtedly have rejected it. His heart shrank at the thought of entering a prison cell again; his only wish now was to die, and hope that his death would mark a change in Irish politics.

While he was in Richmond Barracks, Clarke wrote a note to his wife Kathleen, but she did not receive it until three weeks after the surrender. Dated 30 April, 1916, the last letter she would ever receive from him reads: 'Dear K, I am in better health and more satisfied than for many a day – all will be well eventually – but this is my good-bye and now you are ever before me to cheer me – God bless you and the boys. Let them be proud to follow same path – Seán [MacDiarmada] is with me and McG[arry], all well – they

all heroes. I'm full of pride my love. Yours, Tom'. It was written on a small page torn from a notebook, in pencil, and she
later traced over it in ink in case it would fade. MacDiarmada
had written to her on the other side, addressing her as 'Dear
Cáit'; she was amused by this, as he had never dared address
her as other than 'Mrs Clarke' in all the years they had known
one another. He was being mischievous, knowing she could
not retaliate. His note read: 'I never felt so proud of the boys.
Tis worth a life of suffering to be with them for one hour.
God bless you all, Seán'.[39] Clarke gave his watch to a British
soldier to have the letter delivered.

Tom Clarke was tried by court-martial on Tuesday, 2 May.
He pleaded 'not guilty', on the grounds that the charge
accused him of an act 'being done with the intention and
purpose of assisting the enemy', and that he was not guilty of
that. There was only one witness, 2nd Lieutenant SL King of
the 12th Inniskilling Fusiliers, who testified that he had been
a prisoner in the GPO, and had often seen the prisoner. 'He
appeared to be a person in authority although he was not in
uniform'.[40] Cross-examined by Clarke, he admitted that he
had been well treated in the GPO. The prisoner called no
witnesses on his own behalf, and made no statement, so his
court martial concluded very swiftly.

He returned to the room where the other prisoners were
gathered, and sat on an upturned bucket while they asked
him how it had gone. He had no doubt about his fate on the

next morning: 'The British have been watching their chance
down through the years, and are not going to let it slip now'.
He spoke to them of the future, and of carrying on the fight.
The witness says, 'I realised that Tom Clarke, although he
knew he would be facing the firing squad within the next
six hours, believed in his heart and soul that he and his comrades had defied the British Empire, and that Ireland would
win her freedom'.[41] Clarke was transferred to Kilmainham
Gaol shortly afterwards.

When an escort was sent to bring Kathleen Clarke to Kilmainham to say goodbye to her husband, they found her in
Dublin Castle, where she had been brought earlier that day.
She had been arrested in her home in Fairview, on suspicion
of having been involved in the Rising, and brought to Clontarf police station. She, her maid and a visiting friend were
all taken away, despite Kathleen's vigorous protests. In her
memoir, she reveals that she was leaving behind, uncared-
for, one dog, two cats, and a dozen canaries. Tom had always
been fond of keeping birds, and loved to hear them sing, but
Kathleen could never understand how a man who had been
in jail for so many years could keep a caged bird. She herself bred 'Kerry Blue' dogs, an aggressive breed very popular
with Irish nationalists.

The house was searched, and a sackful of suspicious documents was removed. It had always been rumoured among
the Volunteers that the Clarkes had a large quantity of gold

buried in the back garden, but fortunately the soldiers did not go that far. Madge Daly later said that a quantity of gold had been built into the foundation of a brick arch in the cellar, and this was given to Michael Collins in 1920.

From Clontarf, after her maid and her friend had been released, Kathleen was brought to Dublin Castle, travelling with Arthur Griffith. He had also been arrested, although Sinn Féin had had nothing to do with the Rising. During the journey through the city, she was staggered by how much damage the Rising had caused, and more than once horrified Griffith by shouting encouragement at the groups of Volunteer prisoners who were being brought through the streets. She was put in a cell with several other members of Cumann na mBan, so was able to learn some of what had been going on. They finally got a cup of tea about 9pm. They were frequently disturbed by the soldiers, but tried to get some sleep. Between midnight and 1am, however, Kathleen was informed that her husband wished to see her, and that a car had been sent to bring her to him. She knew what this meant.

The first person she met in Kilmainham was one of the Carmelite priests who were such a strong support to many of the executed rebels. He said that Clarke refused to see him, and wanted Kathleen to change her husband's mind. She said, 'I have never interfered with my husband in anything he thinks right, and I am not going to begin now.'

Clarke said to Kathleen that he had refused to talk to a priest who had urged him to confess his sin. 'I told him to clear out of my cell quickly. I was not sorry for what I had done. I gloried in it and the men who had been with me.'

As Kathleen entered the small, damp cell to which Tom had been moved, the first thing she said to him was 'Why did you surrender? The last thing you said was no surrender'. She could not stop herself – she knew what prison meant to him, and had been certain that he would take care not to survive. He explained that he had hoped to die during the retreat from the GPO, and had subsequently felt he had to go with the majority vote. He told her how well everyone had fought, and broke it to her that her young brother Ned would also die. He wanted her to make clear to everyone that the Germans had not broken any promises; they had only guaranteed a small shipment of arms, and had done that. He also wanted her to work to keep Eoin MacNeill out of any future nationalist movement: 'He is a weak man, but I know every effort will be made to whitewash him'.

At some point, according to a later account Kathleen gave, he talked to her of remarriage. He did not like to think of it, 'but if at any time when life may be very hard for you and you meet a man you think would make things easier for you, let no thought of me stand in the way of marrying again'. Kathleen wrote, 'I said nothing. I knew no man could ever take his place with me. I think he knew, but he felt it a duty to say that'.[42] She was pregnant again, after a seven-year gap, but did not tell him; she felt it would place too great a burden on him.

With difficulty, they talked of their sons. He wanted them to be happy, and to follow in his footsteps, but she pointed out that his death would always shadow their lives, and that children did not always do what their parents wanted. Even at the doorway to execution, Kathleen was still the plain speaker she had always been. He gave her a full description of the fight, the retreat and the surrender. It was a long interview, at least two hours, but Kathleen says, 'I did not miss a word he said. It is burned into my brain'.

She held herself together, afraid that if she showed weakness it would weaken him, but she wondered afterwards if he understood her seeming lack of emotion.

A soldier came in and said 'Time's up', and she had to stand at the cell door while it was locked. 'The sound of that key in that lock has haunted me ever since.' Several accounts say that Clarke was then visited by two priests, Father Columbus and Father Tom Ryan. Possibly he received Communion after all as, according to an article written in 1946, 'he received absolution and Holy Communion from … Father Tom O'Ryan of Goldenbridge … who always felt pride and thankfulness in the thought that it had fallen to his lot to console in his last moments on earth the greatest Fenian of them all'.[43]

On the way out, Kathleen asked about receiving her husband's body for burial, but was told that no orders had yet been received about the disposal of the bodies of the executed men. She was brought back to the Castle and given a cup of tea, and subsequently released at about 6am, with a permit because curfew was in force till 7am. She had to walk home, not having eaten since the previous morning, and could not even eat when she got there. She filled herself a tumbler of wine, although she was a teetotaller; she hoped it might help her sleep, but it only gave her an hour's respite. Later, two of her sisters, Madge and Laura, arrived from Limerick, and were with her that evening when a car came from Kilmainham to take them to say goodbye to their brother Ned, who was to be executed the following morning.

Tom Clarke was executed around 4.15 on the morning of Wednesday, 3rd May, 1916, along with Patrick Pearse and Thomas MacDonagh. The witness statement of a DMP constable, Michael Soughly, says, 'there was great admiration amongst the staff of the jail for the manner in which the executed leaders met their fate, especially Tom Clarke who, notwithstanding his age and frail constitution, expressed his willingness to go before his firing party without a blindfold.'[44] This was not allowed.

Tom Clarke wished to see Kathleen's brother before he died, but Ned Daly was still in Richmond Barracks and could not be brought over in time. However, when he arrived Ned insisted on seeing Tom dead or alive, and was allowed to go into the shed where the three bodies lay, and say a prayer. He was then taken to his own court-martial, and was executed the following day.[45]

Clarke left Kathleen a message for 'the Irish people', later circulated on a memorial card:

'I and my fellow-signatories believe we have struck the first successful blow for Freedom. The next blow, which we have no doubt Ireland will strike, will win through. In this belief we die happy'.

The whole story of the Easter Rising will be gone through in more and more detail as the centenary approaches, and probably for long after. What did they hope to achieve? Was it worth it?

Undoubtedly for Tom Clarke it was worth it; he had worked out his long-planned vengeance against the old enemy, Britain. Despite his age and reclusive manner, this shy, dedicated man had engaged the loyalty and commitment of hundreds of idealistic and enthusiastic younger men, along with money and support from his old Fenian and Clan na Gael comrades, and was able to march to his execution with a sense of fulfilment and an ambition achieved. He knew in his heart that his death would not be the end of the fight.

Tom Clarke's personality is very difficult to evaluate, as it is one of extreme contradictions. A person of intense self-con-

Above: Painting of the Provisional Government. Left to right, seated: Thomas MacDonagh, Tom Clarke, Éamonn Ceannt, Seán MacDiarmada, Joseph Plunkett. Standing, left: Patrick Pearse, and right, James Connolly.
Below: Flag flown over the GPO.

Irish Rebellion - May 1916
The General Post Office, Dublin (Rebel Headquarters) destroyed

Ruins of G.P.O., Dublin, as seen from top of Nelson's Pillar

Above: Damage to the GPO.

Left: The ruins of the GPO, as seen from the top of Nelson's Pillar.

Above: Cumann na mBan who were very active during the Rising and afterwards.

Below: Damage to O'Connell Street.

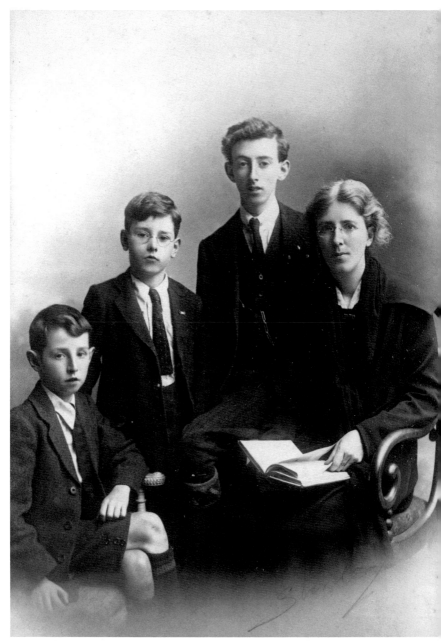

Above: The Clarke family after the Easter Rising, 1916. Left to right: Emmet, Tom junior, Daly, and their mother Kathleen.

Dependents of Executed Leaders May 1916

Mrs Clarke.......Husband executed; three boys left, no assistance
given, as this was her own wish.

Mrs Pearse.......Two sons executed, two? daughters left, £250 given

Mrs MacDonagh....Husband executed, two children left,   £250 given.

Mrs Kent ....Husband executed, one son left.   £250 given.

Mrs O'Hanrahan...Son executed, three daughters left, two
of whom had been previously at business £100 given.

Mrs Connolly.....Husband executed, 5 of family, 3 worked £ 50 given.
1st instalment.

Sean MacDermott,.No dependents.

Con. Colbert   ..No dependents.

Mrs Mallon .....Gets £1 per week.

Joseph Plunkett.. Nil.

Ed, Daly   ......Left mother and sisters, no assistance given.

Mrs Heuston......Son executed, sister left. Got £5 at the time, and a
collection was organised in Limerick by Late Mr Daly
and Miss Daly(members of our Committee)which realised
about £70, and this was handed to Mrs Heuston.
Major MacBride...Nil.   Kent (Cork) nil.   Sir Rodger Casement Nil.

Above: List of dependants to be given aid by the National Aid and
Volunteer Dependants' Fund, 1916.

Above: Seán MacDiarmada.

Opposite: Photographs of the Daly/Clarke families set in a cardboard mount painted by Constance Markievicz while imprisoned in Holloway Jail. Top: Edward Daly and his mother, Catharine; Centre: the Daly sisters and their mother after the Rising; Bottom: Daly Clarke; John Daly, Tom Clarke and Seán MacDiarmada; Tom Clarke junior.

Above: Edward Daly.

trol, the only man to emerge from imprisonment whole and intact in mind and body – even Daly and Egan suffered from ill-health and alcohol problems in later life, probably traceable to their prison experiences – he nonetheless allowed passion to deflect him from his committed path when he met and married Kathleen Daly. His ruling passion remained locked within, a deep commitment to punishing the British Empire for the wrongs it had done to Ireland.

PS O'Hegarty, in his Introduction to Clarke's *Glimpses of an Irish Felon's Prison Life*, asserts that his imprisonment, 'while it certainly strengthened his political faith, left him without bitterness and utterly without that passion for revenge which is ascribed to him'.[46] This does not ring true; he could not have given so many years to building up a revolutionary body, dealing with the inevitable personality struggles and competing egos, attracting the energy and devotion of so many young people to whom his past was a vague rumour, without a deep inner drive. He must occasionally have considered making peace with his history, settling into domestic happiness, making a modest living and watching his sons grow up, but such an urge would have been rejected as weakness, tempting him from the true path. If he had a faith at all, this was his – Britain had to be confronted and shamed, at whatever cost to himself and his family.

It was easy for others to believe that he was without bitterness or anger because he never allowed these to show. While

John Daly, for example, almost made a career of denouncing British brutality, Clarke never willingly spoke of his prison experiences, describing them as 'a bad dream best forgotten', and his stories in *Glimpses of an Irish Felon's Prison Life* are told lightly, with an occasional glance of humour. They are all the more devastating for that lightness of touch. He refused to emphasise his sufferings, but he never forgot them. His wife describes him, in the domestic context, as 'impulsive and quick-tempered', but few outside his closest circle would ever have seen that side of him.[47]

Many of those who worked with or lived with Tom Clarke have left fond recollections of him. He rarely aroused anger or irritation; even those who ultimately disagreed with him, such as McCullough, do not blame him for being intransigent or obstructive – they surmise that he was badly advised, or under MacDiarmada's influence. But Tom Clarke was his own man, and any shortcomings are his own too. He could be suspicious and secretive, occasionally judging people harshly on little evidence, and his trust once lost was lost forever. On the other hand, he always praised work well done, and gave immense encouragement to those who were trying their best.

An anonymous draft for a life of Tom Clarke, now in the National Library of Ireland, describes him as being 'generous, kind and full of fun and humour'. He had a 'quick, decisive manner', and was very selective in his choice of friends. He was a 'most vital force in giving the movement the direction he desired', and John Devoy said of him that in all his long experience, 'he never met a man with the energy and enthusiasm of Tom for national work'.[48]

Tom Clarke was a shy man to meet for the first time, 'so frighteningly shy that sometimes to talk with him was agony', but once he let down his reserve 'he was a man vital with ideas, on fire with force, masterful and confident'.[49] Some of this apparent shyness may have been due to growing deafness. He could seem stern and abrupt on first acquaintance, but in his home, Kathleen insists, he was 'the kindest and the most considerate and thoughtful of men'. However, she adds, 'his wife, his child, nothing counted when Ireland called'.[50]

Epilogue

Dublin city centre lay in ruins. Sixteen men, including Roger Casement in London, were executed for their part in the great adventure. For most of them it had been a matter of several years of preparation, but Tom Clarke's whole life, from his teenage years, had led him to this climax.

314 civilians (of whom 64 were insurgents) had been killed, 2,217 people had been wounded, and 116 British soldiers had died along with thirteen RIC officers and three members of the DMP. John F Boyle, in an early account of the rebellion, states that between 27 April and 4 May 415 people were buried in Glasnevin Cemetery alone, 216 due to fatal gunshot wounds. Thirty of the 415 were unidentified. Boyle comments that 'Numbers were interred in gardens and other burial grounds. Many were burned and buried in debris'.[1] Estimates of the damage caused reached two-and-a-half million pounds, with one and three-quarter million pounds to be paid in compensation.[2]

Dublin Castle's administration had been shattered – Birrell had to resign, and Wimborne was replaced – and the parade of executions began to change the mood of the people. An English writer later commented: 'the Government wavered between the two policies [of conciliation or cruelty], and achieved the usual results of half measures. Within a few weeks popular sentiment in Ireland had completely swung round, and the rebellion was converted … from a disgraceful failure into a glorious success'.[3] Another English writer, more dramatically, agreed with this assessment: 'By the severity of our executions of men who were dreamers and patriots rather than men of evil character, and whose rebellious acts, mad and wicked as they were in effect, had not been inspired by low criminal passions, we made martyrs of them and stirred the burning sympathy of every Irish man and woman and child, we lit the flames of hate in Ireland and stoked its fires'.[4]

The day after Ned Daly's execution, the Clarke home was once again raided by British soldiers. Kathleen and her two sisters went to Richmond Barracks to visit the prisoners, and that evening, she formed the first committee of the Irish Republican Prisoners Dependants' Fund. Tom had left her in charge of £3,100 of IRB money; in her memoir she says, 'When talking to Tom in Kilmainham Gaol, he had told me to use the money I had to relieve distress, but I am sure he had no idea of the thousands of men who would be arrested'.[5] She distributed help and sympathy to the dozens of women who called to her home, many of them desperate for news of their husbands or sons.

The Volunteer Commandants had been instructed to tell their men that Mrs Clarke was to be contacted in case of need, and each Commandant had sent her a list of relevant families, presumably mostly those with young children. However, those lists had been lost in the destruction and the raids, so only temporary relief was given until circumstances could be verified. Kathleen was also in possession of many of the IRB's secrets; several members of the Supreme Council had been told that they were to get in touch with her after the Rising, if they survived, to 'keep up the threads of the organisation'.[6]

On Saturday, leaving the rest of the money with Sorcha MacMahon, a Cumann na mBan member who acted as her second-in-command and would continue the work, Kathleen went down to Limerick to talk to her sons about their father's death: 'they were very sweet and comforting, but still I could not cry'. Emmet, who was only six, said later that he did not know for six weeks that his father had died.[7] The whole Daly family had been shattered. Mrs Daly had little sympathy to spare for her widowed daughter, but focused on her only son's death, grateful that he had died for Ireland and not in a foreign war; she rarely smiled again. Uncle John was devastated at the loss not only of his nephew, but of two of his closest friends.[8] His health was already poor, and he died on 30 June 1916, aged 70.

Kathleen tried to keep some semblance of family life going for her sons; a postcard album belonging to young Emmet contains a card accompanying a birthday gift, 'With loving wishes to my darling Emmet for a Happy Birthday, Mama'. The card is dated 13 August 1916.[9]

The money Clarke had provided soon began to run out, although many families were still in dire need. A public appeal for funds was organised by Kathleen and Miss MacMahon, among others. There was competition from a fund supported by the Irish Parliamentary Party, but both funds ultimately amalgamated as the National Aid and Volunteer Dependants' Fund; the influence of the IPP was fading. Kathleen facilitated this amalgamation, and also worked to reunite Cumann na mBan, which had split briefly on the issue of who had been 'out' or not in Easter Week.

Kathleen drove herself hard for weeks, going down to Limerick every weekend to see her children, until she ultimately collapsed and suffered a miscarriage. She came near to death – indeed her heart stopped briefly – but within a few days she was sitting up in bed, dealing with correspondence. Cumann na mBan continued to administer the fund, which had branches all over Ireland. The list of subscribers grew, and the fund was sustained through flag-selling and other fundraising activities.[10]

Kathleen herself was not in good financial circumstances. Clarke's shop in Parnell Street had been raided by the military after the Rising, and the stock looted or destroyed. The landlord had then taken back the premises, and she could not recover them. She insisted on paying all her husband's business creditors, and newspaper advertisements invited them to contact Henry Lemass, her solicitor; creditors included Gallaher Ltd, MH Gill and Son, and *The Kerryman*. Lemass sent cheques to each of them, and the covering letter said that although Mrs Clarke was under no legal obligation to do so, 'she decided to supplement the money in the Bank [Clarke's business account] to an extent sufficient to pay all the Creditors twenty shillings in the pound and she has forwarded me the necessary funds for this purpose. The Creditors of the Deceased may congratulate themselves that they are dealing with a lady of such high principles…'[11]

About a year after his death, Kathleen received her husband's final legacy. This consisted of £1, 'property of a prisoner',[12] and the spectacle case, pencil, stamp book (with seven stamps) and knife which were in his possession on his execution, which were all sent to his solicitor, Hugh O'Brien Moran.[13]

As the Dependants' Fund grew, it required more professional management, and a Secretary was advertised for in late 1917. By this time those who had been arrested after the Rising had been released, and one of these, Michael Collins, a Volunteer who had fought in the GPO, applied for the post. Kathleen supported his application, but it was understood that his main function was to continue the fight for freedom: 'As Secretary to the NAVDF, he would be free to move about the country without molestation. Everyone would be free to go into the office of the Fund without arousing suspicion, as so many people were seeking help … With his forceful personality, his wonderful magnetism and his organising ability, he had little trouble in becoming a leader'. He reminded her in many ways of Seán MacDiarmada.[14]

Kathleen Clarke remained a political activist for the rest of her life. She saw her role as continuing her husband's fight, and did so at a certain cost to herself and her family. She saw little of her children, who were essentially raised by their aunts in Limerick; they attended St Munchin's Diocesan College there. Her home was raided often, by the British, by the Black and Tans during the War of Independence, by the Free State Army during the Irish Civil War. During one Black and Tan raid, she feared greatly for her son Daly, then sixteen years old, as boys of that age had been shot out of hand before, but after checking whether he was shaving yet, they left him alone. Her children grew used to being dragged out of bed in the middle of the night, even in Limerick, as the Daly home was also a focus of Black and Tan attacks.

In May 1918, after the British government received warnings of a 'German Plot', supposedly a Sinn Féin plan concocted with Germany, Michael Collins warned Kathleen to go on the run, as she was sure to be on the list of suspected persons. She did not believe him, but she was wrong. She was sent to Holloway Jail, London, in the company of Maud Gonne (now the widow of John MacBride) and Constance

Markievicz. She was released on the grounds of ill-health the following February, having suffered a possible heart attack, and then spent seven weeks recovering from the influenza that swept Europe after the end of the First World War. Her son Emmet recalls, 'She told me many years later that I had come to her saying: "Don't leave me; don't leave me". It is possible that she knew I did not get on very well with my aunts and grandmother. That gave her the will to live…'[15]

An Irish parliament, Dáil Eireann, was established by Sinn Féin after it won a majority of seats in the 1918 general election. Kathleen had been elected a member of Dublin Corporation, standing for Sinn Féin, and in 1920 the Corporation acknowledged the authority of the Dáil. When the Dáil established Republican Courts, in opposition to the official British system, Kathleen became a County Court judge, and chair of the Dublin North City judges.

When the Anglo-Irish Treaty of 1921 was proposed, Dáil Éireann split. Kathleen Clarke was one of those who vehemently opposed the Treaty, on the basis that it was not what her husband and brother had died for. She helped the anti-Treaty side during the Civil War. The Daly family initially completely rejected the Treaty and the Irish Free State, but gradually came to terms with the reality. Kathleen was made a Freeman of Limerick on 6 December 1921, and she and her husband share the distinction of being the only married couple on Limerick's Roll of Freemen. In 1923, she opened a tobacconist's shop at 16 D'Olier Street, but this had closed by 1926.[16]

In 1924, Kathleen toured America as her uncle had done. She was seeking Irish-American support for the Dependants' Fund, and also visiting her son Daly, who was in Florida for his health, working as a cab driver. Since she would not have been allowed a passport to visit the United States, she travelled to Canada instead and managed to slip across the border. Daly himself seems to have travelled without any problems, sailing from Southampton on the White Star steamship *Arabic* on 7 September 1921; he was nineteen.

Kathleen was a founder member of Fianna Fáil, the political party established in 1926 by Éamon de Valera, a Volunteer Commandant who had survived the Rising. She was a member of the Senate, Seanad Éireann, from 1928 to 1936; it was then abolished until de Valera produced a new Constitution in 1937, whose limitations on women she strongly opposed. She was a member of Dublin Corporation until 1945, and was Dublin's first woman Lord Mayor from 1939 to 1941, when Fianna Fáil was in government. She often disagreed with government policy, and when an IRA man, Patrick McGrath, was executed for shooting a policeman, she flew flags at half-mast on the Mansion House and City Hall, a very public repudiation of de Valera's stance. She finally resigned from Fianna Fáil in 1943, feeling they were no longer truly nationalist.

In 1935, Kathleen commissioned a Breton author, Louis Le Roux, to write a biography of Tom Clarke. Le Roux received contributions to the book from many participants in the Rising, and Kathleen and her sister Madge gave him a great deal of family material. The book itself is more a hagiography than a biography, which is perhaps to be expected. The publishers, Talbot Press, were a bit wary of it, and, according to Desmond Ryan, who had a long correspondence with Le Roux, 'seriously suggested to delete all serious mention of the IRB from his life. What has Mrs T.C. to say to that?'[17]

Kathleen began to write her memoirs around 1940, and added to them over several years. They were offered to Dents Publishers in 1962, but Dents' solicitors advised them not to publish, because of the possibility of libel. The memoirs went back in the drawer, and she decided that they would not be published until after her death. Kathleen Clarke's memoirs were finally published in 1991, twenty years after her death, by The O'Brien Press, under the title *Revolutionary Woman*.

Patrick Pearse's central role in 1916 meant that he was frequently referred to as President of the Provisional Government in accounts of the Easter Rising. Kathleen Clarke vigorously opposed this every time it was said; in her view, Tom was President, and Pearse's adherents were claiming something that was not true. In a letter of 1961, kept by the historian Leon Ó Broin, she talks about her memoir:

'In regard to the Presidency, I had to handle that carefully, as I think I would be wrong nationally to say exactly what I think, but I can tell you in confidence that Pearse had no more right to sign himself President than I had … There are men now alive who know for a certainty that Tom was President, but who refrain from saying so lest it might in a sense besmirch Pearse … What a lot of people do not know is that Pearse was very ambitious and as vain as a peacock…'

She adds, 'Tom said nothing to me about the Presidency when I was with him in Kilmainham Gaol … as he knew I might blaze about it, he would want to head me off doing so, and I asked all the men … on return from prison if they knew of any change during the week, all knew he went into the GPO as President'.[18] This became something of an *idée fixe* with her, and over the years she irritated many people because she would not let go of it. She never felt Clarke received the recognition he deserved, and fought much longer on his behalf than he would probably have done for himself. She was backed up by her brother-in-law, Éamonn de hÓir, in many letters and lectures over the years. Clarke himself, once asked by her about candidates for the Presidency, had jokingly replied that it would have to be 'someone with a touch of Cromwell in him for the first five years'. Pressed further, he said the only one he could think of 'who would have the knowledge of our enemy, the force and ruthlessness for the position', would be his old friend of Clan na Gael, John Devoy.[19]

In later life Kathleen, still active on numerous committees and hospital boards, lived in Sandymount, Dublin, near to her eldest son Daly and his wife Mary. In 1968 she made a visit to Tom's childhood home, Dungannon, to attend a Golden Jubilee Dinner of the Thomas Clarke Gaelic Football Club. She is described as 'tall and stately with an alert carriage …even at first acquaintance one is aware that this woman is exceptional'. The reporter who interviewed her noted that her conversation always returned to Tom Clarke. He asked about him:

'Did he smoke?'

'Yes, cigarettes.'

'Did he like to go for long walks?'

'How could he and him working in the shop from eight in the morning until 11 o'clock at night.'

She also referred to the many women who had worked for the republican cause, both during the Easter Rising and in the following years: 'They were the salt of the earth, and they have never received the credit they so richly deserved'. While in Dungannon, she was the guest of Clarke's old friend, Billy Kelly.[20]

She continued to receive cards and letters from men and women who had known herself and her husband, reminiscing about the past. One letter, dated 14 April 1964, from a man called Michael Lennon, brings her back to Maple Farm in Long Island. Lennon had visited the farm, now called Mayflower Farm and owned by a man from Texas, and had found that it was to be deeded to the Presbyterian Church for spiritual retreats. He adds, 'I felt as I was coming away that there should be a memorial at this place for Clarke. Maybe some future generation will repair the omission.'[21]

Daly Clarke, eldest son of Tom and Kathleen, married Mary Byrne, whose father had been in the RIC, in 1952, and worked with the Irish Hospitals Sweepstakes. He died in 1971, aged sixty-nine; he and Mary had no children.

The second son, Tom, married Maureen Kennedy of Limerick in 1939. He managed Daly's Bakery for many years, and was later a director of the Irish Life Assurance Company. He stood for election for Fianna Fáil during the 1940s, but without success. He died in 1988, aged eighty; he and Maureen had no children.

The youngest son, Emmet, trained as a doctor and became a psychiatrist. Despite all his mother's efforts, he could not find employment in Ireland, and emigrated to England, where he worked for the National Health Service. He married Ellen Mullaney, an Irish nurse, in 1955, and moved from Nottingham to Liverpool in 1961. He died in 2005, aged ninety-five. He and Ellen had two sons, Tom and Emmet; Tom is married, with two sons.

In 1965, Kathleen Clarke went to live with her son Emmet and his family in Liverpool, probably to be near her only grandchildren. She died there on 19 September 1972, aged ninety-four, and was given a state funeral in Dublin. She is buried in Glasnevin Cemetery. A copy of her will is now in the National Library, Dublin. Her property is divided between Daly and Emmet, with no mention of Tom; he and his mother were never close.[22]

Eighteen months after Tom Clarke's execution, Mrs Clarke senior was to lose her only surviving son, Alfred. On 8 November 1917, newspapers reported that Alfred Clarke, a Dublin Corporation timekeeper, had been missing for some days. It was noted that he was the brother of Thomas Clarke, executed in 1916.[23] About two weeks after his disappearance, Alfred's body was recovered in the Grand Canal. A verdict of accidental death was brought in, with a rider calling attention to 'insufficient lighting arrangements' along the canal.[24] A fund was set up to help his widow Emily and their five children, James, John, Nora, Emily and Thomas.

Five years later, Mrs Clarke senior died. Her death revived memories of the Easter Rising, as the death notice made clear her connection with it:

'CLARKE (Baldoyle) – 16 July 1922, at her residence, Clarke's Villa, Baldoyle, MARY CLARKE, mother of the late Tom Clarke, executed at Kilmainham Jail, 1916. R.I.P.'

A representative of the Dáil Cabinet attended her funeral. Dublin Corporation passed a vote of condolence to Alderman Mrs Clarke on the loss of her mother-in-law.[25]

Clarke's sister Hannah died on 11 October 1950 in the Hospice for the Dying, Harold's Cross and was buried with her parents in Glasnevin Cemetery.

The *Irish Press* describes her as a staunch nationalist, who had sheltered many men on the run during the War of Independence, and her funeral was attended by representatives of the Old Cumann na mBan, Old IRA and Old Fianna, as well as a representative of the President.[26]

Clarke's other sister, Maria, had died during the 1920s. Tom and Kathleen had kept in contact with her for at least twenty years after her marriage in 1901, and references in their letters indicate that Teddy Fleming had difficulty keeping a job.[27] As far as is known, Maria and Teddy had only one child, Edward. In 1966, Edward James Fleming wrote to An Taoiseach, Éamon de Valera, congratulating him on the fiftieth anniversary of the Easter Rising, and introducing himself as a nephew of Tom Clarke.[28] Nothing more is known of this branch of the Clarke family.

There are several memorials to Tom Clarke in Ireland, but nothing in Dublin, where he spent so much of his life. Limerick City has done most to honour him; the massive monument on Sarsfield Bridge portrays Tom Clarke, his brother-in-law Edward Daly and another Limerick Volunteer, Con Colbert, in bronze, beside a personified Éire with broken manacles, and a depiction of the Proclamation.

In 1966, when the 1916 leaders were honoured during

the celebrations of the Centenary of the Easter Rising, Tom Clarke's name was given to Dundalk railway station. One of the high-rise towers in Ballymun, County Dublin, was also named after him, but this has since been demolished.

A plaque to the Clarke family can be found in a disused Church of Ireland church in Clogheen, County Tipperary, where Tom Clarke's mother was born.

There is, apparently, a plaque commemorating Tom Clarke at the farm in Manorville, Long Island, New York, where he and Kathleen spent several very happy years.

NOTES

CHAPTER 1

1 University College Dublin Archives Department, Desmond Ryan Papers, LA 10/408.

2 Military records relating to James Clarke, National Archives, Kew, WO 97/1313/236.

3 The witnesses were John Flynn and John Gordon. Her family may not have attended the ceremony, as Catholics were discouraged from entering Protestant churches.

4 'Notes for a Life of Tom Clarke', National Library of Ireland, Tom Clarke and Kathleen Clarke Papers, Ms 49,355/8.

5 Gerard MacAtasney confirms that Tom was not born on the Isle of Wight, as stated in Le Roux's biography and many other sources. Hurst Castle was at the other side of the Solent: Gerard MacAtasney, *Tom Clarke, Life, Liberty, Revolution*, The History Press (2013), p13, note 4.

6 Louis Le Roux, *Tom Clarke and the Irish Freedom Movement*, Talbot Press (1936), p8.

7 'Notes for a Life of Tom Clarke', as above, note 4.

8 Military records, as above, note 2.

9 This looks as though he re-enlisted, but the matter is unclear. James Clarke received a final discharge from the military 'on account of old age' in 1886, having served a total of 38 years and 102 days. He was fifty-six years old. He seems to have drawn his Chelsea pension throughout.

10 In the Census records of 1911, Tom's mother Mary, widowed and living in Dublin, indicates that eight children had been born to her, of whom four survived. The entry has been crossed out, but is quite legible. The other births cannot be traced.

11 Le Roux, *Tom Clarke*, p10.

12 Sean McGarry, BMH WS 368.

13 MacAtasney, *Tom Clarke*, pp3–5. Billy Kelly's memoir is in the O'Fiaich Library and Archive Armagh, where it is included among the Papers of Father

Louis O'Kane.

14 Census of Ireland, 1881.

15 University College Dublin, Archives Department, Desmond Ryan Papers, LA 10/408.

16 Le Roux, *Tom Clarke*, pp15-16.

17 Sean McGarry, BMH WS 368.

18 *Belfast Morning News*, 18 August 1880.

19 MacAtasney, *Tom Clarke*, pp4-5.

20 Le Roux, *Tom Clarke*, p17.

21 'Notes for a Life of Tom Clarke', as above, note 4.

22 Le Roux, *Tom Clarke*, pp18-19.

23 Le Roux, *Tom Clarke*, p23.

24 William J Kelly, BMH WS 226.

25 Robert Emmet, whose brother Thomas had been a leader of the 1798 United Irishmen rebellion, planned a revolution for July 1803. However, when an ammunition store exploded in Dublin, he had to rise prematurely, and few people followed him. Emmet was hanged and beheaded on 20 September 1803.

26 *The Brooklyn Eagle*, Sunday 5 March 1882.

27 John Merriman, *The Dynamite Club*, JR Books, London 1990, p73.

28 Johann Most, *The Science of Revolutionary Warfare – A Manual of Instruction in the Use and Preparation of Nitroglycerine, Dynamite, Gun-Cotton, Fulminating Mercury, Bombs, Fuses, Poisons, etc., etc.*, Chicago (1885).

29 Le Roux, *Tom Clarke,* p20.

30 Sean McConville, *Irish Political Prisoners, 1848-1922* – Theatres of War, Routledge (2003), p348.

31 MacAtasney, *Tom Clarke*, pp66-7.

32 Le Roux, *Tom Clarke*, pp24-5.

33 Henri Le Caron [Thomas Miller Beach], *Recollections of a Spy: Twenty-Five Years in the Secret Service*, London (1892), p240

34 Le Caron, *Recollections of a Spy*, p275.

35 Percy H Fitzgerald, FSA, *Chronicles of Bow Street Police Office, Vol II*, London (1888), pp361-72.

36 MacAtasney, *Tom Clarke*, p9.

37 Le Roux, *Tom Clarke*, p29.

38 Le Caron, *Recollections of a Spy*, p242.

39 Le Caron, *Recollections of a Spy*, p241.

40 Christy Campbell, *Fenian Fire: The British Government Plot to Assassinate Queen Victoria*, London (2002), p141.

41 Le Caron, *Recollections of a Spy*, pp242-3.

42 UCD Archives, Desmond Ryan Papers, LA 10/47; letter from Madge Daly dated 10 March 1953.

43 *Brooklyn Eagle*, Saturday 5 May 1883.

44 *Brooklyn Eagle*, Monday 18 June 1883.

45 Le Roux, *Tom Clarke,* pp32-3.

46 National Library of Ireland, Desmond Ryan papers, 'Letters to Le Roux', Ms 44,684/5.

47 Le Roux, *Tom Clarke*, pp32-5.

CHAPTER 2

1 For background on the British penal system I am indebted to Dr Barry Vaughan, who lent me his unpublished PhD Thesis, *Power/Knowledge – Untying the Knot, an examination of a penological method, submitted to the University of Warwick, 1997.*

2 M. Ignatieff, *A Just Measure of Pain: The Penitentiary in the Industrial Revolution,* Macmillan (1979), pp72-3.

3 Colonel Sir Edmund Du Cane, *The Punishment and Prevention of Crime,* London (1885), pp56-69.

4 Rev. D. Nihill, *Prison Discipline and its Relation to Society and Individuals* (1839).

5 Charles Dickens, *American Notes,* London (1842). I am indebted to Tony Farmar for this reference.

6 Thomas J. Clarke, *Glimpses of an Irish Felon's Prison Life,* Dublin (1922), pp4-5.

7 National Library of Ireland, Tom Clarke and Kathleen Clarke Papers, Ms 49,354/2.

8 William J Kelly, BMH WS 226.

9 MacAtasney, *Tom Clarke,* p15.

10 Clarke, *Glimpses,* pp14-15, 18-19.

11 Clarke, *Glimpses,* pp68-70.

12 Clarke, *Glimpses,* p8.

13 Clarke, *Glimpses,* p85.

14 Clarke, *Glimpses,* p23.

15 Minutes of Evidence taken before the visitors of Her Majesty's Convict Prison at Chatham as to the Treatment of certain prisoners convicted of Treason Felony, H.C., 1890, National Archives, Kew. A copy of the report is also among the Clarke Papers in the National Library of Ireland, Ms 49,354/1.

16 All quotes are from Chatham Report, as above, note 15.

17 University College Dublin, Archives Department, Desmond Ryan Papers, Letter from Madge Daly, 1947, LA10/47.

18 Clarke, *Glimpses,* p33.

19 Clarke, *Glimpses,* p30.

20 National Archives, Kew, Chatham Enquiry File, Ms LPAAA.

21 National Library of Ireland, 'Tom Clarke and Kathleen Clarke Papers', Ms 49,354/2.

22 Le Roux, *Tom Clarke,* p50.

23 National Library of Ireland, Desmond Ryan Papers, 'Letters to Le Roux', Ms 44,684/5, writer unidentified.

24 MacAtasney, *Tom Clarke,* p36.

25 He had earlier given Mrs Clarke £10, but advised her to tell the Amnesty committee that it had been a smaller amount, for fear of her son Alfred asking for some of it. Alfred seems to have been a difficult family member: two letters, John Daly to Hannah Clarke, July 1897, copies in possession of Helen Litton.

26 MacAtasney, *Tom Clarke,* pp38-9.

27 Clarke, *Glimpses,* p66, pp93-4.

28 NLI, Clarke Papers, Ms 49,354/2.

CHAPTER 3

1 *Irish Daily Independent,* 30 September 1898.

2 *Kathleen Clarke, Revolutionary Woman* (ed. Helen Litton), The O'Brien Press (2008 edition), p31.

3 Louis Le Roux, *Tom Clarke and the Irish Freedom Movement,* Talbot Press (1936), p53.

4 National Library of Ireland, Desmond Ryan Papers, 'Letters to Le Roux', Ms 44,684/3; letter from Emma Hart, dated 30 April 1935.

5 National Library of Ireland, Tom Clarke and Kathleen Clarke Collection, Ms 49,355/13, anonymous notes for a life of Tom Clarke (1934).

6 Gerard Conlon, *Proved Innocent*, Penguin Books (1990), p232.

7 Gerard MacAtasney, *Tom Clarke: Life, Liberty, Revolution,* Merrion/ Irish Academic Press (2013), pp45-7.

8 MacAtasney, *Tom Clarke*, pp47-8.

9 The household consisted of John Daly, his sister Laura (Lollie), his mother Margaret, his sister-in-law Catharine and her nine children: Eileen, Margaret (Madge), Kathleen, Laura, Caroline (Carrie), Annie, Nora and Edward. Catharine's husband Edward Daly had died in 1890, five months before the birth of his son.

10 *Kathleen Clarke*, p31.

11 NLI, Clarke Collection, Ms 49,351/1; letters dated 26 March 1899; 10 June 1899.

12 *Irish Daily Independent*, 30 September 1898.

13 NLI Ms 49,354/4.

14 NLI Ms 49,351/1, letter dated 1 April 1899, from 5 St Anthony's Road, Kilmainham, Dublin.

15 NLI Ms 49,351/1, letters dated 4 May 1899, June 1899, 27 August 1899.

16 NLI Ms 49,351/1, letters dated 4 April 1899, 10 June 1899.

17 MacAtasney, *Tom Clarke*, pp50-1.

18 NLI Ms 49,351/1, letter dated 5 June 1899.

19 Interview with Kathleen Clarke, *[Tipperary] Guardian*, 14 October 1972.

20 Michael Foy and Brian Barton, *The Easter Rising*, The History Press (2011 edition), p13.

21 NLI Ms 49,354/1, letters dated September 1899; 17 August 1899.

22 Maud Gonne, whose father had been in the British Army, became a lifelong activist in the cause of Irish nationalism, and was also active in land agitation. In 1900 she founded Inghinidhe na hÉireann ('Daughters of Ireland'), a women's nationalist movement. She was for many years the muse and love-interest of the poet WB Yeats.

23 MacAtasney, *Tom Clarke*, p51.

24 Le Roux, *Tom Clarke*, p58.

25 MacAtasney, *Tom Clarke*, p155, letter dated 9 February 1900, from 363 West 36th Street, New York.

26 MacAtasney, *Tom Clarke,* p161, letter from 1750 Second Avenue, New York.

27 NLI, Tom Clarke and Kathleen Clarke Papers, Ms 49,352/2.

28 MacAtasney, *Tom Clarke*, pp174-5, letter dated 22 January 1901, from 1305 Brook Avenue, The Bronx.

29 *Kathleen Clarke*, p36.

30 Radio interview by Donncha Ó Dulaing with Emmet Clarke, broadcast on Radio Éireann, 7 April 1991.

31 NLI, as above, note 27.

32 NLI, as above, note 27, letter dated 5 January 1901.

33 MacAtasney, *Tom Clarke*, p170.

34 NLI, as above, note 27.

35 NLI, as above, note 27, letter dated 18 April 1901.

36 *Kathleen Clarke*, p37.

37 *Kathleen Clarke,* p29.

38 Almost all the addresses where the Clarkes lived during these years have been replaced by later development.

39 *Kathleen Clarke*, p30.

40 American-Irish Historical Society, 991 Fifth Avenue, New York 10028: Daniel Cohalan Papers, Box 2, Folder 27.

41 *Kathleen Clarke*, p40.

42 MacAtasney, *Tom Clarke*, p59.

43 Le Roux, *Tom Clarke*, pp62-3.

44 NLI, Desmond Ryan Papers, 'Letters to Le Roux', Ms 44,684/3; letter from John Carroll, n.d.

45 Le Roux, Tom Clarke, pp69-70.

46 *Kathleen Clarke*, pp41-2.

47 Le Roux, *Tom Clarke*, pp68-9.

48 *Kathleen Clarke*, p44.

49 NLI, Tom Clarke and Kathleen Clarke Papers, Ms 49,352/3, letters dated 21 January 1904, 23 June 1904.

50 Boston College, John J Burns Library, Tom Clarke Collection, MS 01-07.

51 *Kathleen Clarke*, p47.

52 MacAtasney, *Tom Clarke*, p193.

53 *Kathleen Clarke*, p48.

54 MacAtasney, *Tom Clarke*, pp63-4.

55 It has been suggested that Devoy wanted Clarke in Dublin to replace Patrick Neville Fitzgerald, an IRB man trusted by the Clan, who had died in October 1907.

56 NLI, Tom Clarke and Kathleen Clarke Papers, Ms 49,352/6, folder 1, letter dated 9 January 1908.

57 NLI, as above, note 56, letters dated 20 January 1908, 6 January 1908; MacAtasney, *Tom Clarke*, pp202-3.

58 MacAtasney, *Tom Clarke*, p196, p202.

59 NLI, as above, note 56, letter dated 18 January 1908.

60 *Kathleen Clarke,* p51.

61 MacAtasney, *Tom Clarke*, p199.

62 NLI, as above, note 56, letter dated 3 March 1908.

63 MacAtasney, *Tom Clarke*, p204.

64 NLI, as above, note 56.

65 *Kathleen Clarke*, p52.

66 NLI, as above, note 56, letters dated 18 February 1908, 25 February 1908.

67 NLI, as above, note 56, folder 2, letter dated March 1908.

68 NLI, as above, note 56, folder 2, letter dated 29 March 1908.

69 NLI, as above, note 56, folder 2, letter dated 1 February 1908.

70 Joseph Robins, *The Miasma: Epidemic and Panic in Nineteenth-century Ireland,* Institute of Public Administration (1995), p33.

71 *Kathleen Clarke*, p53.

CHAPTER 4

1 Denis McCullough, BMH WS 915.

2 Louis Le Roux, *Tom Clarke and the Irish Freedom Movement*, Talbot Press (1936), pp111-12.

3 PS O'Hegarty, quoted in anonymous draft of 'Life of Tom Clarke', NLI Ms 49,355/13.

4 Le Roux, *Tom Clarke*, pp84-5.

5 Gerard MacAtasney, *Sean MacDiarmada, The Mind of the Revolution*, Drumlin Publications (2004), p41.

6 John Devoy, *Recollections of an Irish Rebel*, Irish University Press (1969), pp392-3.

7 Born Constance Gore-Booth in 1868, she married the Polish count Casimir Markievicz, an artist, in 1900. They had one daughter, and later separated. Constance, who was later a close friend of Kathleen Clarke, became an officer in the ICA, and was imprisoned after the Rising. She remained all her life a strong activist in labour and nationalist circles, and was the first woman elected an MP to the British Parliament in 1918, although she did not take her seat. She died in poverty in Dublin in 1927, mourned by the poor among whom she had lived.

8 Seán McGarry, BMH WS 368.

9 Le Roux, *Tom Clarke*, p89.

10 Gerard MacAtasney, *Tom Clarke, Life, Liberty, Revolution*, Merrion/Irish Academic Press (2013), p72.

11 *Kathleen Clarke, Revolutionary Woman* (ed. Helen Litton), O'Brien Press (2008 edition), p56.

12 Thomas Barry, BMH WS 1.

13 Pat McCartan, BMH WS 766.

14 Joseph Gleeson, BMH WS 367.

15 MacAtasney, *Tom Clarke*, pp73-4.

16 *Kathleen Clarke*, p58.

17 Le Roux, *Tom Clarke*, p113.

18 MacAtasney, *Tom Clarke*, p67.

19 Willam O'Brien and Desmond Ryan (eds.), *Devoy's Postbag*, C.J. Fallon Ltd (2 vols, 1948, 1953), Vol II, p395, letter dated 10 February 1911.

20 National Library of Ireland, Tom and Kathleen Clarke Papers, Ms 49,351/8.

21 NLI Ms 49,351/2, letter dated 16 July 1912.

22 Ronan Fanning, *Fatal Path: British Government and Irish Revolution, 1910-1922*, Faber and Faber Ltd (2013), p55.

23 O'Brien and Ryan, *Devoy's Postbag, Vol II*, p412, letter dated 25 June 1913.

24 Fanning, *Fatal Path*, p95.

25 Robert Smyllie, 'An Irishman's Diary', *Irish Times*, 19 July 1943.

26 American-Irish Historical Society, 991 Fifth Avenue, New York 10028, Daniel Cohalan Collection, Box 2, Folder 18.

27 Éamonn de hÓir, *Memoirs* (unpublished), p118: Courtesy of Siobháin de hÓir.

28 Richard Connolly, BMH WS 523.

29 Garry Holohan, BMH WS 328.

30 Le Roux, *Tom Clarke*, pp131-2.

31 Letter from Emmet Clarke to author, 10 May 1995.

32 Denis McCullough, BMH WS 916.

33 MacAtasney, *Tom Clarke*, p78.

34 Bulmer Hobson, BMH WS 81.

35 *Kathleen Clarke,* pp64-5.

36 Seamus Daly, BMH WS 360.

37 National Library of Ireland, Leon Ó Broin Collection, 'Materials collected by Padraig Ó Maidin for a biography of Tom Clarke', Ms 31696.

38 O'Brien and Ryan, *Devoy's Post Bag*, Vol II, p448, letter dated 3 June 1914.

39 Robert Brennan, BMH WS 766.

40 De hÓir, *Memoirs,* p118.

CHAPTER 5

1 Quoted in Garret FitzGerald, 'The Significance of 1916', *Studies*, Spring 1966.

2 Austen Morgan, *James Connolly, A Political Biography,* Manchester University Press (1986), p168.

3 Fanning, Ronan, *Fatal Path: British Government and Irish Revolution, 1910-1922,* Faber and Faber Ltd (2013) pp137-8.

4 American-Irish Historical Society, Cohalan Collection, Box 2, Folder 18.

5 Fanning, *Fatal Path*, p133.

6 Fanning, *Fatal Path,* p67.

7 University College Dublin, Archives Dept, RIC Reports P59/1; P59/2.

8 Robert Brennan, BMH WS 779.

9 University College Dublin, Archives Dept., p16, letter from E.G. O'Kerwin, dated 14 May 1914.

10 Liam Ó Briain, 'The Historic Rising of Easter Week – 1916', *Voice of Ireland*, p132.

11 MacAtasney, *Tom Clarke*, p81.

12 Patrick McCartan, BMH WS 766.

13 Ben Novick, *Irish Nationalist Propaganda during the First World War*, Four Courts Press (2001), pp229-30.

14 *Kathleen Clarke, Revolutionary Woman* (ed. Helen Litton) The O'Brien Press (2008 edition), pp70-1.

15 *Kathleen Clarke*, p72.

16 *Kathleen Clarke*, pp75-6

17 Denis McCullough, BMH WS 766.

18 Diarmuid Lynch, BMH WS 4.

19 University of Limerick, Glucksman Library, Daly Papers, Box 2, Folder 52, letter dated June 1915.

20 *Kathleen Clarke,* p79.

21 Seán McGarry, BMH WS 368.

22 Joseph Gleeson, BMH WS 367.

23 *Kathleen Clarke*, p81.

24 Brian Barton, *Secret Court Martial Records of the Easter Rising,* The History Press (2010 edition), p309.

25 MacAtasney, *Sean MacDiarmada*, p90.

26 *Kathleen Clarke*, pp83-4.

27 National Library of Ireland, Tom Clarke and Kathleen Clarke Collection, Ms 49,353/3.

28 Quoted in Seán McGarry, BMH WS 368.

29 Sydney Gifford Czira, BMH WS 909.

30 Joseph O'Rourke, BMH WS 1244.

31 NLI, Tom Clarke and Kathleen Clarke Papers, Ms 49,355/4.

32 Barton, *Secret Court Martial Records*, p309.

33 WJ McCormack, *Dublin 1916, The French Connection,* Gill and Macmillan (2012), p83.

34 Devoy, *Recollections,* p458.

35 David Thornley, 'Patrick Pearse', *Studies* (Spring 1966), pp10-19.

36 Charles Wyse Power, BMH WS 420.

37 NLI, Tom Clarke and Kathleen Clarke Papers, Ms 49,352/6, letter dated January 1908.

38 NLI, as above, note 78; letter dated February 1908.

39 NLI, as above, note 78; letters dated April 1908.

40 NLI, as above, note 78; letter dated 25 May 1908.

41 NLI, Tom Clarke and Kathleen Clarke Papers, Ms 49,351/8, letter dated 24 April 1912.

42 MacAtasney, *Tom Clarke,* p245.

43 Kathleen Clarke, draft witness statement for BMH, 1950 (later withdrawn) A copy was in Kathleen Clarke's archive until 2006, when the archive was sold at auction; notes made by Helen Litton, 1991.

44 Letter from Emmet Clarke to Helen Litton, 10 May 1995.

45 Emmet Clarke, interview with Donncha Ó Dulaing, Radio Éireann broadcast, 7 April 1991.

46 NLI, Tom Clarke and Kathleen Clarke Papers, Ms 49, 355/12, Anonymous, 'Notes for a Life of Tom Clarke' (1934).

CHAPTER 6

1 National Library of Ireland, Tom Clarke and Kathleen Clarke Papers, Anonymous draft of 'Life of Tom Clarke' (1934), NLI Ms 49,355/13.

2 Louis Le Roux, *Tom Clarke and the Irish Freedom Movement,* Talbot Press (1936), p123; Lorcan Collins, *Sixteen Lives: James Connolly,* The O'Brien Press (2012), p208; carbon copy of original letter in Boston College, John J Burns Library, Tom Clarke Collection, MS 01-07.

3 Seán McGarry, quoted in Desmond Ryan, *The Rising, The Complete Story of Easter Week,* Golden Eagle Books (1949), p57.

4 Seán McGarry, BMH WS 368.

5 Éamonn de hÓir, Memoirs (unpublished), p187; courtesy of Siobháin de hÓir.

6 Éamonn Dore (de hÓir), BMH WS 153.

7 Michael Foy and Brian Barton, *The Easter Rising,* The History Press (2011 edition), p18.

8 Denis McCullough, BMH WS 915/916.

9 Seamus Daly, BMH WS 360

10 Ronan Fanning, *Fatal Path: British Government and Irish Revolution 1910-1922,* Faber and Faber Ltd (2013), p23, p150.

11 University College Dublin, Archives Dept., Mulcahy Papers, P7: RIC Reports.

12 National Archives, Kew, London, RIC Reports CO 904/23, letter dated 14 March 1916.

13 Anonymous Nun, Mater Hospital, BMH WS 463.

14 *Kathleen Clarke, Revolutionary Woman (ed. Helen Litton),* The O'Brien Press (2008 edition), p94.

15 Boston College, Tom Clarke Collection, Box 9.

16 Eamonn de hOir, Miscellanies (unpublished), letter to Desmond Ryan dated 28 May 1961, p9; courtesy of Siobháin de hOir.

17 National Library of Ireland, Ms 31,700; reference courtesy of Gerard MacAtasney.

18 *Kathleen Clarke,* p98.

19 Kitty O'Doherty, BMH WS 355.

20 Denis McCullough, BMH WS 915.

21 Piaras Béaslaí, BMH WS 261.

22 Bulmer Hobson, BMH WS 81.

23 *Kathleen Clarke,* pp98-9.

24 Patrick O'Daly, BMH WS 220.

25 FX Martin, quoted in Austen Morgan, *James Connolly, A Political Biography,* Manchester University Press (1988), p182.

26 *Revolutionary Woman,* pp99-100.

27 John O'Connor, *The 1916 Proclamation,* Anvil Books (1999 edition), pp40-7.

28 *Revolutionary Woman,* p92, p101.

29 Charles Townshend, *Easter 1916, The Irish Rebellion,* Allen Lane/Penguin Group (2005), pp131-3.

30 Seán T O Ceallaigh, BMH WS 1765.

31 Eithne McSwiney, BMH WS 119.

32 *Revolutionary Woman,* pp103-4.

33 O'Doherty, WS 355.

34 Seamus Daly, BMH WS 360.

35 O'Ceallaigh, WS 1765.

36 Liam Ó Briain, BMH WS 3.

37 McCullough, WS 915/916.

38 Ó Briain, WS 3.

39 Gerard MacAtasney, *Tom Clarke, Life, Liberty, Revolution*, Merrion/Irish Academic Press (2013), p88.

40 Pat McCartan, BMH WS 766.

41 *Revolutionary Woman*, pp105-6.

42 Foy and Barton, *Easter Rising*, pp65-6.

43 Townshend, *Easter 1916*, pp138-40.

44 Piaras Béaslaí, BMH WS 261.

45 *Revolutionary Woman*, pp107-11.

46 Maureen Wall, 'The Plans and the Countermand', in K B Nowlan (ed.), *The Making of 1916*, Dublin (1969), p218.

47 Garry Holohan, BMH WS 328.

48 Patrick O'Daly, BMH WS 220.

49 William O'Brien, *The Irish Revolution and How it Came About*, p245.

50 Foy and Barton, *Easter Rising*, p188.

51 William Daly, BMH WS 291.

52 Catherine Rooney (née Byrne), BMH WS 658.

53 Brian Barton, *Secret Court Martial Records of the Easter Rising*, The History Press (2010 edition), p152.

54 Dick Humphreys, 'Easter Week in the GPO', published in Keith Jeffrey, *The General Post Office and the Easter Rising*, Irish Academic Press (2006), pp140-56; also published as *'A Rebel's Diary'* in *The Belvederian*, Vol IV, No. 3, 1917.

55 Seán MacEntee, *Episode at Easter*, Dublin (1966), p146.

56 NLI, Clarke Papers

57 *Kathleen Clarke*, p113.

58 Townshend, *Easter Week*, p214.

59 Desmond FitzGerald, *Desmond's Rising*, Liberties Press (2006), p136.

60 Desmond Ryan, *The Rising, The Complete Story of Easter Week*, Golden Eagle Books (1949), p139.

61 Frank O'Connor, *The Big Fellow*, Poolbeg Press (1979), p28.

62 Seán McGarry, BMH WS 368.

63 Leslie Bean de Barra (née Price), in Donncha Ó Dulaing, *Voices of Ireland,* The O'Brien Press (1984), pp95-8.

64 De hÓir, *Memoirs,* pp164-5.

65 Ernie O'Malley, 'A Student in the Rising', in Roger McHugh, *Dublin 1916,* Arlington Books (1966), p130.

66 National Library of Ireland, Rankin, MS 22,251 acc. 3537.

67 Joe Good, BMH WS 388.

68 De hÓir, *Memoirs,* pp168-70.

69 FitzGerald, *Desmond's Rising,* p150.

70 NLI, Rankin, Ms 22,251.

71 Leslie Price (Bean de Barra), BMH WS 1754.

72 Le Roux, *Tom Clarke,* p222.

73 Foy and Barton, *The Easter Rising,* pp261-2.

74 Max Caulfield, *The Easter Rebellion,* Gill and Macmillan (1995 edition), p183.

75 Clair Wills, *Dublin 1916: The Siege of the GPO,* Profile Books (2009), pp54-5.

76 James Ryan, 'The GPO', *Capuchin Annual* (1942), p222.

77 Humphreys, in Jeffrey, *The GPO,* pp149-50.

78 Aoife de Burca, BMH WS 359.

79 De Burca, WS 359.

80 De hÓir, *Memoirs,* p173.

CHAPTER 7

1 These included my grandfather, Captain James O'Sullivan of the First Battalion, who subsequently was one of those who surrendered in Moore Street. Sentenced to death, he was reprieved and interned. In 1918 he married Laura, sister of Edward Daly and Kathleen Clarke.

2 Michael Foy and Brian Barton, *The Easter Rising,* The History Press (2011 edition), p198.

3 Interview in Donncha Ó Dulaing, *Voices of Ireland,* The O'Brien Press (1984), p101.

4 Desmond FitzGerald, *Desmond's Rising: Memoirs 1913 to Easter 1916,* Liberties Press (1968), p154.

5 Charles Saurin, BMH WS 288.

6 Fergus Burke, BMH WS 694.

7 Kathleen Clarke, draft witness statement for BMH (later withdrawn); notes taken by Helen Litton, 1991

8 Éamonn de hÓir, *Memoirs* (unpublished), p174; courtesy of Siobháin de hOir.

9 Joseph Good, BMH WS 388.

10 Sean McLoughlin, BMH WS 290.

11 Saurin, WS 288.

12 Desmond Ryan, *The Rising, The Complete Story of Easter Week*, Golden Eagle Books (1949), p71.

13 Foy and Barton, *The Easter Rising*, p205.

14 Ruth Taillon, *When History Was Made: The Women of 1916*, Beyond the Pale Publications (1996), p87.

15 McLoughlin, WS 290.

16 'In Memory of Elizabeth O'Farrell', National Commemoration Committee, The Workers' Party (1981).

17 Joseph Connell, *Dublin in Rebellion*, Lilliput Press (2009 edition), pp178-9.

18 Honor O Brolcháin, *Sixteen Lives: Joseph Plunkett*, The O'Brien Press (2012), p395.

19 Desmond Ryan, BMH WS 724.

20 Saurin, WS 288.

21 De hÓir, *Memoirs*, p177.

22 De hÓir, *Memoirs* . p177; de hÓir states that Clarke, MacDiarmada and Ned Daly were stripped and abused.

23 Julia Grenan, 'Story of the Surrender', *The Catholic Bulletin* (June 1917).

24 Piaras Mac Lochlainn, *Last Words*, Kilmainham Jail Restoration Society (1971), p40.

25 Mac Lochlainn, *Last Words*, p40.

26 Foy and Barton, *The Easter Rising*, p210.

27 Saurin, WS 288.

28 William Whelan, BMH WS 369.

29 De hÓir, *Memoirs*, p178.

30 Ryan, *The Rising*, p258.

31 Piaras Béaslaí, *Michael Collins*, Phoenix Publishing Co. Ltd. (2 vols) (1926),

Vol. 1, p122.

32 Liam Ó Briain, in PF Mac Lochlainn, *Last Words,* Kilmainham Jail Restoration Society (1971), p44 (originally in Irish).

33 Joseph Gleeson, BMH WS 367.

34 De hÓir, *Memoirs,* p179.

35 Mac Lochlainn, *Last Words,* pp41-2.

36 Ó Dulaing, *Voices of Ireland,* p101.

37 Maeve Cavanagh McDowell, BMH WS 270.

38 Kathleen Clarke, 'A Character sketch of Tom Clarke', NLI, Tom Clarke and Kathleen Clarke Papers, Ms 49,355/12.

39 *Kathleen Clarke, Revolutionary Woman* (ed. Helen Litton), The O'Brien Press (2008 edition), p164.

40 Brian Barton, *Secret Court Martial Records of the Easter Rising, The History Press (2010 edition),* p159.

41 Gerald Doyle, BMH WS 1511.

42 Kathleen Clarke, draft BMH statement, as above, note 7.

43 Brian O'Higgins, '*Soldiers of 1916: Greatest of All',* Wolfe Tone Annual (1946), pp37-8.

44 Michael Soughly, BMH WS 189.

45 Helen Litton, *Sixteen Lives: Edward Daly,* The O'Brien Press (2013), pp171-83.

46 Tom Clarke, *Glimpses of an Irish Felon's Prison Life,* Dublin (1922), ppxvi-xvii.

47 Kathleen Clarke, 'Character Sketch', as above, note 38.

48 National Library of Ireland, Tom Clarke and Kathleen Clarke Papers, 'Notes for a Life of Tom Clarke' (1924), Ms 49,355/13.

49 Donagh MacDonagh, 'Tom Clarke', *An Cosantóir* (April 1966), pp 187-98.

50 Kathleen Clarke, draft BMH statement, as above, note 7.

EPILOGUE

1 John F. Boyle, *The Irish Rebellion of 1916: A Brief History of the Revolution and its Suppression,* London (1916).

2 Joseph Connell, *Dublin in Rebellion, A Directory 1913-1923,* Dublin (revised edition, 2009).

3 W Alison Phillips, *The Revolution in Ireland 1906-23*, London (1923).

4 Philip Gibbs, Preface to Hugh Martin, *Ireland in Insurrection, An Englishman's Record of Fact*, London (1921)

5 *Kathleen Clarke, Revolutionary Woman,* The O'Brien Press (2008 edition), p145.

6 Joseph Gleeson, BMH WS 367.

7 Emmet Clarke, radio interview with Donncha Ó Dulaing, broadcast on Radio Éireann, 7 April 1991.

8 *Kathleen Clarke*, pp151-5.

9 John J Burns Library, Boston College, Tom Clarke Collection, Box 7.

10 *Kathleen Clarke*, pp165-70.

11 Letter from Henry Lemass, Solicitor, Parliament Chambers, 31 Parliament Street, Dublin, 8 March 1917. Details of Tom Clarke's estate are in NLI, Tom Clarke and Kathleen Clarke Papers, 49,355/8. The estate was finally wound up on 17 April 1918.

12 Cash Book, 'Prisoners' Effects', WO 35/69/2, National Archives, Kew, London.

13 Copy letter in possession of Helen Litton.

14 *Kathleen Clarke*, p177.

15 Letter from Emmet Clarke to author, 1 April 1996.

16 *Kathleen Clarke*, p275.

17 National Library of Ireland, Desmond Ryan Papers, 'Letters to Le Roux', Ms 44,693.

18 P. Ó Maidin collection, Leon Ó Broin Papers, National Library of Ireland, Ms 31696, letter dated 5 June 1961.

19 Kathleen Clarke, Notes for BMH witness statement (withdrawn), notes made by Helen Litton, 1991.

20 The *Dungannon Observer*, 17 February 1968.

21 Copy letter sent by Emmet Clarke to Helen Litton. Lennon published a series of articles in the *Irish Times* in early 1949, entitled 'The Easter Rising from the Inside'.

22 National Library of Ireland, Tom Clarke and Kathleen Clarke Papers, Ms 49,357/5.

23 *Irish Independent*, 8 November 1917. I am very grateful to Linda Clayton, member of the Association of Professional Genealogists in Ireland, who

researched the Clarke family for me.

24 *Freeman's Journal*, 21 November 1917.

25 *Irish Independent*, 25 July 1922.

26 *Irish Press*, 12 October 1950.

27 Gerard MacAtasney, *Tom Clarke, Life, Liberty, Revolution,* Merrion/IAP (2013), pp185-6.

28 University College Dublin, Archives Dept, Éamon de Valera Papers, P150/470.

BIBLIOGRAPHY

Tom Clarke was for a long time the 'forgotten man' in the history of the Easter Rising, and very little was written specifically about him, although of course he turns up in every history of the period. He himself wrote a series of articles about his prison years, and these were collected into a book, *Glimpses of an Irish Felon's Prison Life*, published in 1922.

In 1935 his widow, Kathleen, commissioned a biography from the Breton writer Louis Le Roux, and she and her sister Madge Daly provided Le Roux with most of the material. The resultant book, *Tom Clarke and the Irish Freedom Movement* (Talbot Press) contains a good deal of first-hand information, but is not what would today be considered a proper critical biography.

Kathleen Clarke wrote her own memoir in the 1940s, and this was published by The O'Brien Press in 1991, almost twenty years after her death, under the title *Revolutionary Woman: Kathleen Clarke 1878-1972*. As a woman's memoir of the period, it attracted a good deal of interest, and also served to bring Tom Clarke's role more strongly into focus.

Further attention was stimulated by the auction sale of Kathleen Clarke's extensive archive, in Dublin in 2006, after the death of her last surviving son Dr Emmet Clarke. Fortunately the bulk of the correspondence and other documents contained in this archive were bought by the National Library of Ireland, and the 'Tom Clarke and Kathleen Clarke Papers' are now available for research.

The most recent publication on Tom Clarke, *Tom Clarke, Life, Liberty, Revolution* by Gerard MacAtasney (Merrion/Irish Academic Press, 2013) contains a very useful, if brief, biography of Clarke, but focuses mainly on the wonderful cache of letters held by the NLI. MacAtasney's aim was to reveal the man behind the stiff portrait most people know. Tom Clarke's voice is very clear in these letters, and one can follow the course of his political thinking and of his private life.

Original Sources

American-Irish Historical Society, 991 Fifth Avenue, New York 10028

John J Burns Library, Boston College

Archives Department, University College Dublin

Bureau of Military History, Cathal Brugha Barracks, Rathmines, Dublin

National Library of Ireland, Dublin

National Archives, Kew, London

Ryan Papers, UCD Archives

Daly Collection, Glucksman Library, University of Limerick

Printed Publications

Barton, Brian, *Secret Court Martial Records of the Easter Rising*, The History Press (2010 edition)

Béaslaí, Piaras, *Michael Collins* (2 vols), Phoenix Publishing Co., Dublin (1926)

Boyle, John F, *The Irish Rebellion of 1916: A Brief History of the Revolution and its Suppression*, London (1916)

Campbell, Christy, *Fenian Fire: The British Government Plot to Assassinate Queen Victoria*, London (2002)

Caulfield, Max, *The Easter Rebellion*, Gill and Macmillan (1995 edition)

Clarke, Kathleen, (ed. Helen Litton), *Kathleen Clarke, Revolutionary Woman*, The O'Brien Press (2008 edition)

Clarke, Thomas J, *Glimpses of an Irish Felon's Prison Life*, Maunsel & Roberts Ltd (1922)

Collins, Lorcan, *Sixteen Lives: James Connolly*, The O'Brien Press (2012)

Conlon, Gerard, *Proved Innocent*, Penguin Books (1990)

De hÓir, Éamonn, *Memoirs*, unpublished Ms

De hÓir, Éamonn, *Miscellanies*, unpublished Ms

Devoy, John, *Recollections of an Irish Rebel*, Irish University Press (1969)

Dickens, Charles, *American Notes*, London (1842)

Du Cane, Colonel Sir Edmund, *The Punishment and Prevention of Crime*, London (1885)

Fanning, Ronan, *Fatal Path: British Government and Irish Revolution, 1910-1922*, Faber and Faber Ltd (2013)

FitzGerald, Desmond, *Desmond's Rising*, Liberties Press (2006)

FitzGerald, Garret, 'The Significance of 1916', *Studies* (Spring 1966)

Fitzgerald, Percy, FSA, *Chronicles of Bow Street Police Office* (2 vols), London (1888)

Foy, Michael and Barton, Brian, *The Easter Rising*, The History Press (2011 edition)

Grenan, Julia, 'Story of the Surrender', *The Catholic Bulletin* (June 1917)

Humphreys, Dick, 'Easter Week in the GPO', in Keith Jeffrey, *The General Post Office and the Easter Rising*, Irish Academic Press (2006)

Ignatieff, M, *A Just Measure of Pain: The Penitentiary in the Industrial Revolution*, Macmillan (1979)

Jeffrey, Keith, *The General Post Office and the Easter Rising*, Irish Academic Press (2006)

Le Caron, Henri [Thomas Miller Beach], *Recollections of a Spy: Twenty-Five Years in the Secret Service*, London (1892)

Le Roux, Louis, *Tom Clarke and the Irish Freedom Movement*, Talbot Press Ltd (1936)

MacAtasney, Gerard, *Sean MacDiarmada, The Mind of the Revolution*, Drumlin Publications (2004)

MacAtasney, Gerard, *Tom Clarke, Life, Liberty, Revolution*, Merrion/Irish Academic Press (2013)

McConville, Sean, *Irish Political Prisoners, 1848-1922 – Theatres of War*, Routledge (2003)

McCormack, W.J., *Dublin 1916, The French Connection*, Gill and Macmillan (2012)

MacDonagh, Donagh, 'Tom Clarke', *An Cosantóir* (April 1966)

MacEntee, Sean, *Episode at Easter*, Dublin (1966)

McHugh, Roger, *Dublin 1916*, Arlington Books (1966)

Mac Lochlainn, Piaras, *Last Words*, Kilmainham Jail Restoration Society (1971)

Martin, Hugh, *Ireland in Insurrection, An Englishman's Record of Fact*, London (1921)

Merriman, John, *The Dynamite Club*, JR Books, London (1990)

Minutes of Evidence taken before the visitors of Her Majesty's Convict Prison at Chatham as to the Treatment of certain prisoners convicted of Treason Felony, H. C. (1890)

Morgan, Austen, *James Connolly, A Political Biography*, Manchester University

Press (1986)

Most, Johann, *The Science of Revolutionary Warfare – A Manual of Instruction in the Use and Preparation of Nitroglycerine, Dynamite, Gun-Cotton, Fulminating Mecury, Bombs, Fuses, Poisons, etc., etc.,* Chicago (1885)

Nihill, Rev. D, *Prison Discipline and its Relation to Society and Individuals* (1839)

Novick, Ben, *Irish Nationalist Propaganda during the First World War,* Four Courts Press (2001)

O'Brien, William and Ryan, Desmond (eds.), *Devoy's Postbag,* C.J. Fallon Ltd (2 vols, 1948, 1953)

Ó Briain, Liam, 'The Historic Rising of Easter Week– 1916', in W G Fitzgerald (ed.), *The Voice of Ireland, A Survey of the Race and Nation from All Angles,* Virtue and Co. Ltd., Dublin and London, 1922

O Brolcháin, Honor, *Sixteen Lives: Joseph Plunkett,* The O'Brien Press (2012)

O'Connell, Joseph EA, *Dublin in Rebellion, A Directory 1913-1923,* Lilliput Press (2009 edition)

O'Connor, Frank, *The Big Fellow,* Poolbeg Press (1979)

O'Connor, John, *The 1916 Proclamation,* Anvil Books (1999 edition)

Ó Dulaing, Donncha, *Voices of Ireland,* The O'Brien Press (1984)

[O'Farrell, Elizabeth] 'In Memory of Elizabeth O'Farrell', National Commemoration Committee, The Workers' Party (1981)

O'Higgins, Brian, 'Soldiers of 1916', *Wolfe Tone Annual* (1946)

O'Malley, Ernie, 'A Student in the Rising', in R McHugh, *Dublin 1916,* Arlington Books (1966)

Phillips, W Alison, *The Revolution in Ireland 1906-23,* Longmans (1923)

Robins, Joseph, *The Miasma, Epidemic and Panic in Nineteenth-Century Ireland,* Institute of Public Administration, Dublin (1995)

Ryan, Desmond, *The Rising, The Complete Story of Easter Week,* Golden Eagle Books (1949)

Ryan, James, 'The GPO', *Capuchin Annual* (1942)

Taillon, Ruth, *When History was Made: The Women of 1916,* Dublin (1996)

Thornley, David, 'Patrick Pearse', *Studies* (Spring 1966)

Townshend, Charles, *Easter 1916, The Irish Rebellion,* Allen Lane/Penguin Group (2005)

Vaughan, Barry, *Power/Knowledge – Untying the Knot, an examination of a penological method*, PhD thesis to University of Warwick (1997), unpublished

Vaughan, WE (ed.), *A New History of Ireland Vol. VI: Ireland Under the Union II, 1870-1921*, Dublin (1996)

Wall, Maureen, 'The Plans and the Countermand' in KB Nowlan (ed.), *The Making of 1916*, Dublin (1969)

Wills, Clair, *Dublin 1916: The Siege of the GPO*, Profile Books (2009)

Index